VECTOR + RASTER FUN

WITH

fashion design

PART II : RASTERS

JOANNE SHERROW

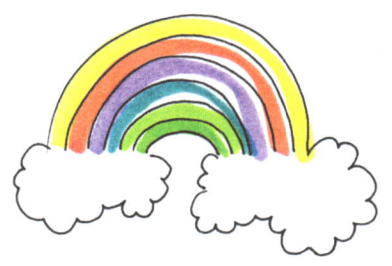

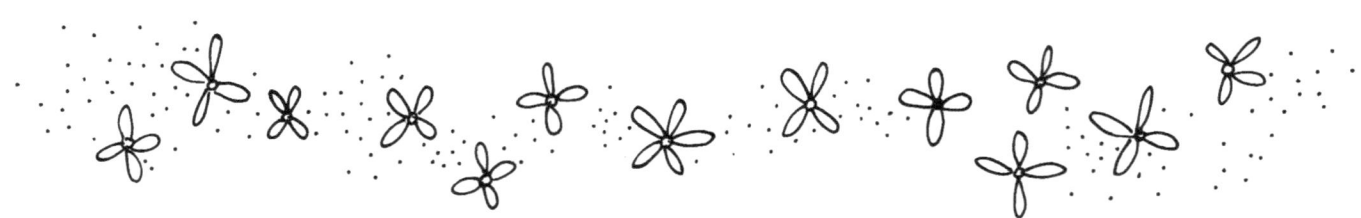

ISBN # 978-0-9826341-0-3

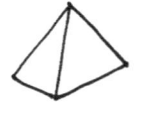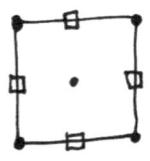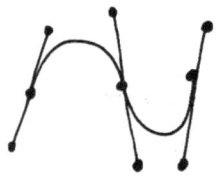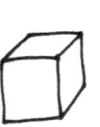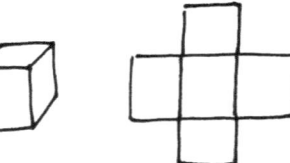

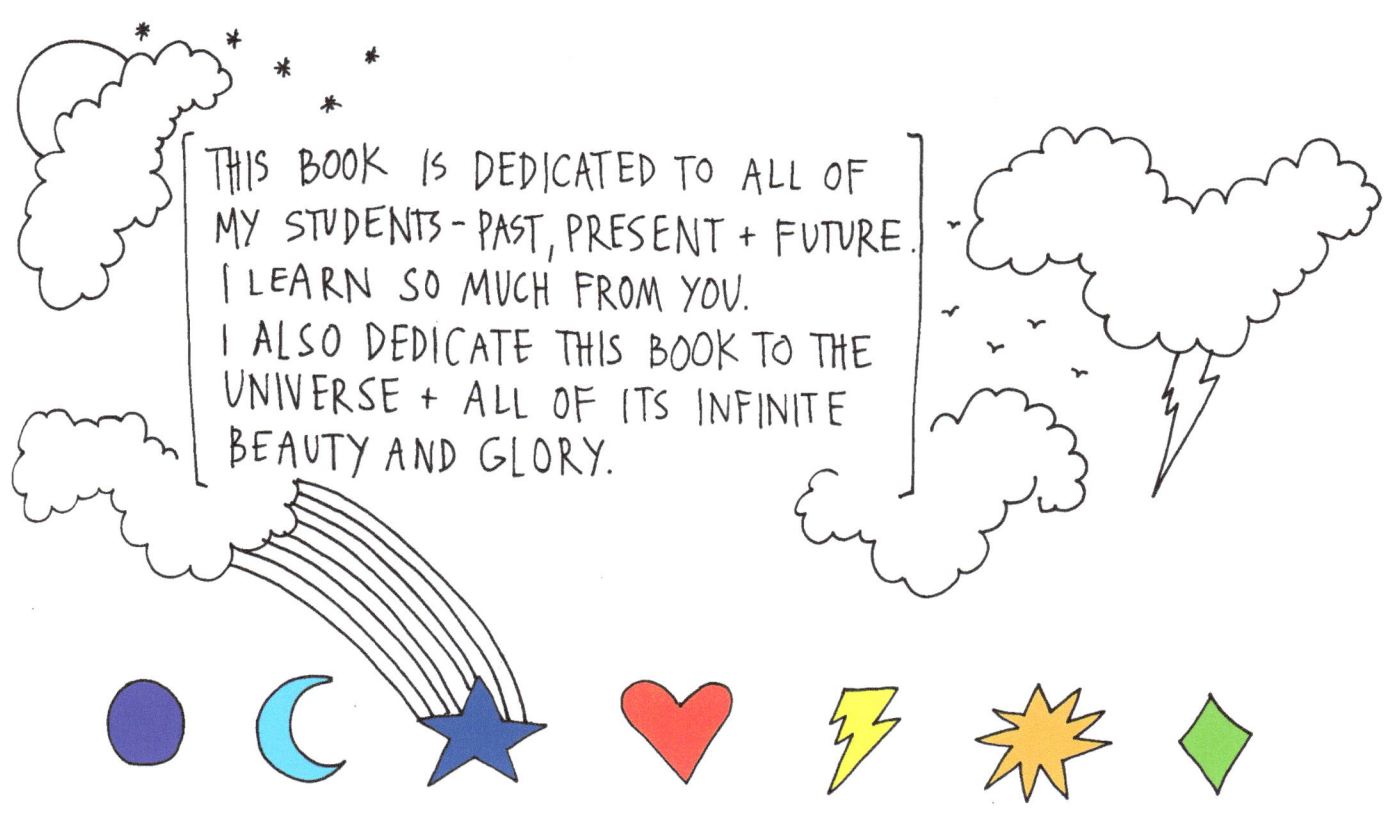

THIS BOOK IS DEDICATED TO ALL OF MY STUDENTS – PAST, PRESENT + FUTURE. I LEARN SO MUCH FROM YOU.
I ALSO DEDICATE THIS BOOK TO THE UNIVERSE + ALL OF ITS INFINITE BEAUTY AND GLORY.

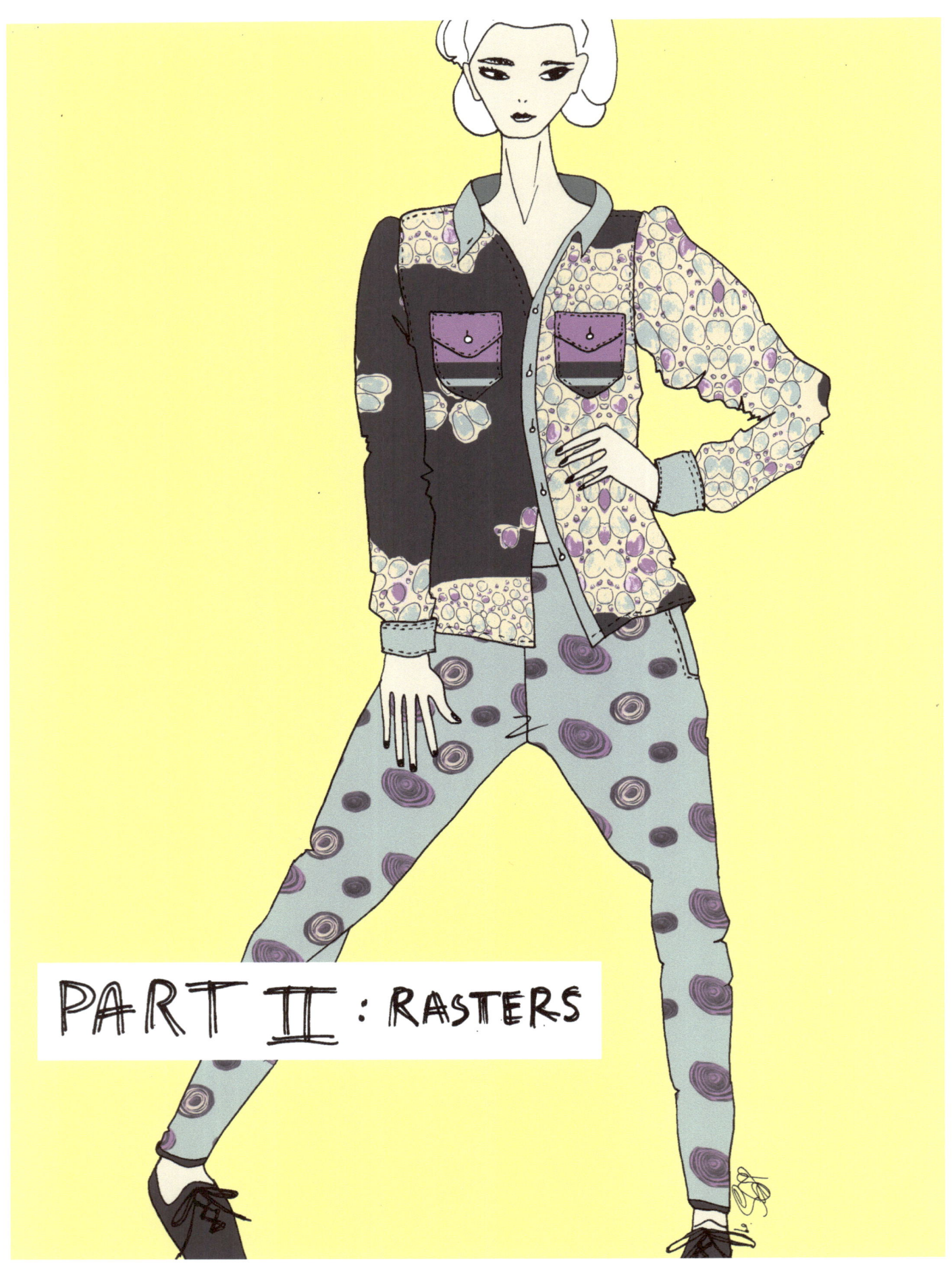

PART II : RASTERS

♥♥ TABLE OF CONTENTS ♥♥

INTRODUCTION TO PART II.

LIKE THE FIRST BOOK IN THIS TWO PART SERIES, I AM WRITING FOR STUDENTS WHO ARE TAKING MY DIGITAL DESIGN CLASSES AT PARSONS, F.I.T, AND 3RD WARD. HOWEVER, THIS BOOK IS ALSO A GOOD ONE FOR THOSE WHO ARE NEW TO THE DIGITAL WORLD OF DESIGN AND ARE MOTIVATED AND EXCITED(!) TO BE SELF TAUGHT IN THESE COMPUTER APPLICATIONS. MY BOOKS OFFER AN ALTERNATIVE TO BOOKS ON THIS SUBJECT OF DRY, TYPESET, HYPER-TECHNICAL, CAR MANUAL-STYLE ILK. STEP-BY-STEP INSTRUCTIONS IN COMBINATION WITH ILLUSTRATIONS + CUMULATIVE EXERCISES HELP YOU TO PROGRESS QUICKLY AND FEEL CONFIDENT WITH THE PROGRAM. A POSITIVE ATTITUDE IS KEY HERE (AND WHEN LEARNING ANYTHING NEW). OTHER THAN ATTITUDE, THE MOST IMPORTANT SKILLS TO BRING TO THE COMPUTER TABLE ARE GOOD COLOR SENSE, DRAWING ABILITY AND TALENT. SO IN ADDITION TO LEARNING C.A.D. (COMPUTER AIDED DESIGN), BE SURE TO KEEP UP YOUR EYE FOR BEAUTY AND DRAWING HAND BY KEEPING A BOOK WITH DOODLES, SKETCHES, NOTES, STICKERS, PHOTO + MAGAZINE CLIPPINGS. THIS WILL BE A GREAT SOURCE OF INSPIRATION WHEN YOU ARE READY TO WORK ON THAT MAGNIFICENT COLLECTION OF YOURS, BE IT TEXTILES FOR WALLPAPER OR AN URBAN SWIMSUIT COLLECTION. MOST OF ALL HAVE FUN WITH ALL OF THIS!

—JOANNE SHERROW
AUGUST 2009 ♡

VECTORS + RASTERS. WHAT'S THE DIFFERENCE?

A VECTOR IS RESOLUTION INDEPENDENT
A RASTER IS RESOLUTION DEPENDENT

VECTORS: LINES (STRAIGHT)
ANCHOR POINTS
TANGENTS (HANDLES)
CURVED LINES
CARTESIAN COORDINATE SYSTEM

vectors - WE CAN MOVE + TRANSFORM THESE NON-DESTRUCTIVELY.
A SMOOTH LINE IN A VECTOR IMAGE WILL ALWAYS
BE A SMOOTH LINE.

RASTERS: PIXELS (VERY SMALL SQUARES)
HOW SMALL? DEPENDS ON RESOLUTION
PRINTED MATERIAL IS 300 D.P.I. (P.P.I.)
SO... EACH PIXEL IN THIS INSTANCE
IS 1/300" (BECAUSE WE HAVE 300 PIXELS PER INCH)

rasters - WHEN WE TRANSFORM THESE IMAGES BY SCALING OR
SKEWING, PHOTOSHOP PERFORMS INTERPOLATION WHERE
EXTRA COLORS MAY BE ADDED AND PIXELS BECOME
DISTORTED. THE IMAGE MAY BECOME FUZZY, HAZY
OR A STAIR-STEPPING LOOK MAY OCCUR.

ILLUSTRATOR - WORKS WITH VECTORS, MAINLY... BUT
(YOU CAN RASTERIZE THE VECTORS HERE TOO.
YOU CAN VECTORIZE THE RASTERS FROM
PHOTOSHOP OR THE WEB.)

PHOTOSHOP - WORKS WITH RASTERS
WHEN USING IMAGES FOR THE WEB, USE 72 P.P.I.
WHEN PRINTING IMAGES ON PAPER OR FABRIC,
USE 300 P.P.I.

RASTER 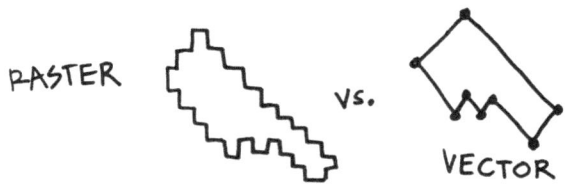 VS.
VECTOR

1

THE SELECTION TOOLS

BEFORE YOU CAN MAKE CHANGES TO A GROUP OF PIXELS / 1 OR MORE PIXELS IN AN IMAGE, PHOTOSHOP NEEDS TO KNOW WHAT EXACTLY YOU WANT TO CHANGE. HOW DO WE ACCOMPLISH THIS? BY CREATING A SELECTION AROUND AN AREA OF PIXELS. THIS SELECTION IS SOMETIMES REFERRED TO AS "DANCING ANTS" OR "MARCHING ANTS" EVEN "BLINKING ANTS" (YOU GET THE POINT). THERE ARE A FEW TOOLS IN PHOTOSHOP THAT WILL MAKE SELECTIONS. THEY ARE:

(1) THE MARQUIS TOOL

THE RECTANGULAR MARQUIS (FOR SQUARES + RECTANGLES)

THE ELIPTICAL MARQUIS (FOR CIRCLES + ELIPSES)

HOW DOES THIS WORK? CLICK ON THE ARTBOARD + DRAG WITH THE MOUSE TO ENLARGE THE SELECTION

* HINT! HOLD DOWN THE SHIFT KEY FOR PERFECT SQUARES AND PERFECT CIRCULAR SELECTIONS

(2) THE LASSO TOOLS (YEE HAW!)

THE LASSO - THIS TOOL WILL CREATE MORE FREE FORM SELECTIONS

THE LASSO WORKS LIKE THE MARQUIS, CLICK AND DRAG TO CREATE AN ORGANIC SHAPE.

POLYGON LASSO - GOOD FOR ANGULAR SELECTIONS BY CLICKING WITH THE MOUSE + LETTING GO A FEW TIMES YOU WILL CREATE A POLYGON

POINT # 1 IS THE ORIGIN HOVER OVER THE POINT TO CLOSE THE SELECTION. YOU WILL SEE AN "O" ASSOCIATED WILL THE TOOL ICON. "O" = ORIGIN

MAGNETIC LASSO - FOR EXISTING IMAGES CLICK CLICK CLICK AROUND AN IMAGE WITH A CONTRASTY BACKGROUND. THIS TOOL WILL ISOLATE IMAGE FROM BACKGROUND

* WHAT #1 + #2 HAVE IN COMMON IS THIS: BOTH CAN BE USED TO MAKE SELECTIONS OVER TOP OF EXISTING IMAGES OR A CANVAS OF SOLID WHITE PIXELS.

THE SELECTION TOOLS

(3) NEXT LET'S HAVE A LOOK AT A SELECTION TOOL THAT SELECTS SOLELY BASED ON COLOR. THIS TOOL IS CALLED "THE MAGIC WAND" (THE 3RD SELECTION TOOL)

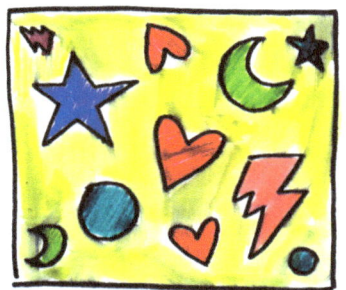

FIG. 1

SAY WE HAVE A NICE REPEAT PATTERN SUCH AS FIGURE 1. IF I WANT TO MAKE A SELECTION AROUND THE PINK HEARTS WE ARE NOT GOING TO USE THE LASSO TOOL. WE WILL HOWEVER USE THE WAND.

* FIRST! TAKE NOTE F THE CONTROL PANEL:

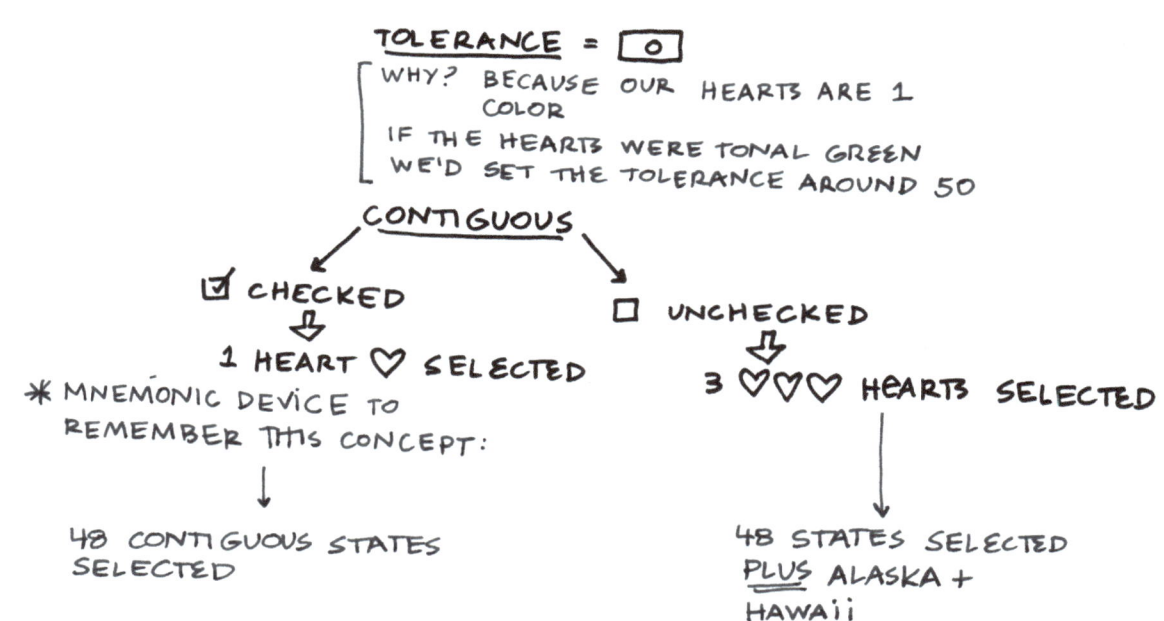

SETTINGS

TOLERANCE = [0]
- WHY? BECAUSE OUR HEARTS ARE 1 COLOR
- IF THE HEARTS WERE TONAL GREEN WE'D SET THE TOLERANCE AROUND 50

CONTIGUOUS

☑ CHECKED
⇩
1 HEART ♡ SELECTED

* MNEMONIC DEVICE TO REMEMBER THIS CONCEPT:
↓
48 CONTIGUOUS STATES SELECTED

☐ UNCHECKED
⇩
3 ♡♡♡ HEARTS SELECTED
↓
48 STATES SELECTED PLUS ALASKA + HAWAII

EXERCISE: CREATE A 5"X 5" SQUARE CANVAS FILL THE BACKGROUND WITH A SOLID COLOR. METHODICALLY CREATE MOTIFS TO MIMIC FIGURE 1. THEN EXPERIMENT CREATING SELECTIONS USING THE WAND. USE THE LASSO TO CREATE SHAPE AND EDIT < FILL USING FOREGROUND COLORS.

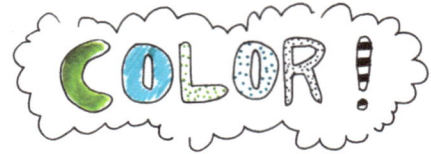

COLOR!

COLOR _IS_ ONE OF THE MOST IMPORTANT PARTS OF YOUR DESIGN. SO... LET'S CREATE A COLOR STORY BEFORE WE DO ANYTHING ELSE.

WHERE CAN WE FIND COLOR THEMES?
1. PULL THEM OUT OF THIN AIR
2. CREATE A COLLAGE _OR_ COLOR MOOD BOARD, SCAN IN, THEN USE THE EYE DROPPER TOOL TO SAMPLE EXISTING COLOR
3. IMPORT WEB IMAGES, SCAN IN YOUR ARTWORK, USE COLORS FROM DIGITAL PHOTOS

NEXT... WE STORE COLOR IN THE SWATCHES PALETTE
      WINDOW > SWATCHES
      WE ADD A COLOR VIA

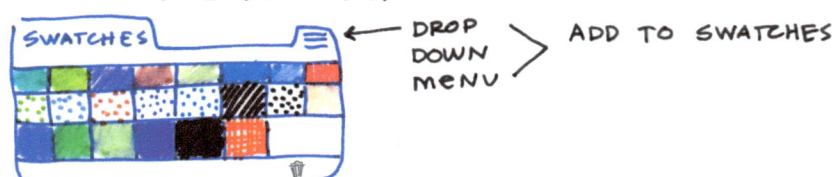
← DROP DOWN MENU > ADD TO SWATCHES

IF WE WANT TO DELETE A COLOR, WE DRAG THE SWATCH TO THE TINY TRASH CAN IN THE LOWER RIGHT

NAMING THEM: GIVE YOUR COLORS FUN NAMES BE CREATIVE!

SAVING THEM: DROP DOWN MENU > SAVE SWATCHES
      MYCOLORS.ACO ⟶ FILE EXTENSION

OPENING THEM: DROP DOWN MENU < REPLACE SWATCHES
      CHOOSE MYCOLORS.ACO
      VOILA!

SAMPLE THEM: (FROM IMAGES) USE THE EYEDROPPER
      DROP DOWN 🔽 > ADD TO SWATCHES

EXERCISE: CREATE 2 COLOR STORIES
      WITH 12 SWATCHES EACH
      8 MAIN COLORS
      4 ACCENT COLORS
      NAME ALL COLORS AND SAVE!

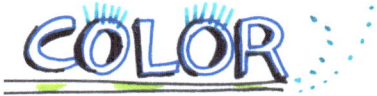COLOR

HOW DO WE ADD COLOR TO A SELECTED AREA OF PIXELS? IN A FEW WAYS:

BUT FIRST! LET'S PUT COLOR INTO THE TOOL BOX

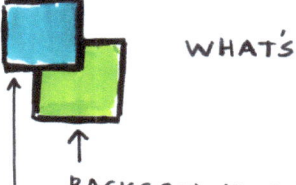

WHAT'S THIS?

BACKGROUND COLOR

FOREGROUND COLOR

PREPARATION:
SET IT UP BEFORE PERFORMING THE FUNCTION...

I. EDIT < FILL
    USE: FOREGROUND COLOR <u>OR</u>
          BACKGROUND COLOR

II. USE THE "PAINT BUCKET" TOOL
    SETTINGS: TOLERANCE = [0]
              CONTIGUOUS = ☑ OR ☐ (DEPENDING ON THE SITUATION)

III. USE AN ADJUSTMENT LAYER
    (MY SNEAKY WAY OF INTRODUCING THE LAYERS PALETTE)
        WINDOW > LAYERS
        CLICK ON THE BLACK + WHITE COOKIE ICON ◑
        CHOOSE SOLID
        PICK A COLOR FROM YOUR PALETTE
        OK!
    * NOW WE HAVE A SELECTION OF PIXELS
       IN A SEPARATE LAYER

INTRODUCING "THE COLOR PICKER"
  DO THIS: CLICK ONCE ON THE "FOREGROUND COLOR"
         WE NOW SEE A DIALOG BOX WHERE YOU MAY

H 1) CHOOSE A HUE (ROY G BIV) FROM THE RAINBOW (USE THE SLIDER...)

V 2) CHOOSE A LEVEL OF LIGHTNESS OR DARKNESS
      TOP = LIGHTEST
      BOTTOM = DARKEST

S 3) CHOOSE AN INTENSITY LEVEL (AKA SATURATION)
      RIGHT = MOST INTENSE
      LEFT = LEAST INTENSE

    WHEN HAPPY WITH YOUR COLOR, OK!

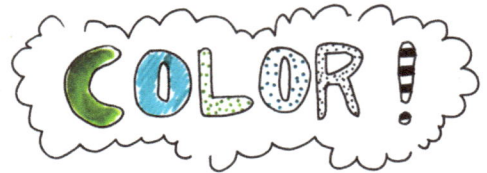

COLOR!

NOW LET'S MAKE A NICE PRINTOUT OF YOUR COLOR PALETTES
WE'LL USE OUR KNOWLEDGE OF MARQUIS TOOLS + COLOR FILLS
TO CREATE A LAYOUT.

FIRST! CLICK THE [ ] RECTANGULAR MARQUIS TOOL

   SETTINGS: FIXED SIZE   1" X 1"

CREATE A 17" X 11" CANVAS

FILE > NEW

W = 17"

H = 11"

RESOLUTION = 300 P.P.I.

COLOR MODE = RGB 8 BITS

VIEW < RULERS {THIS WILL ALLOW FOR GUIDES}

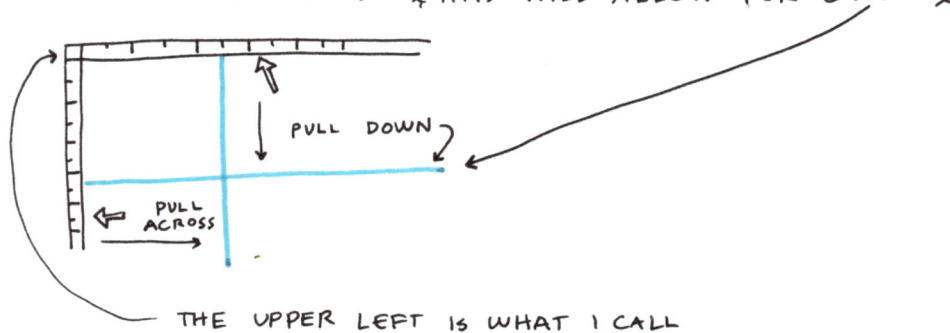

PULL DOWN

PULL ACROSS

THE UPPER LEFT IS WHAT I CALL
"NO MANS LAND" GUIDES WILL NOT
BE GENERATED FROM THIS AREA.

SO... GIVE YOURSELF GUIDES FOR MARGINS +
   3 HORIZONTAL GUIDES (EQUIDISTANT)
   5 VERTICAL GUIDES (ALSO EQUIDISTANT)

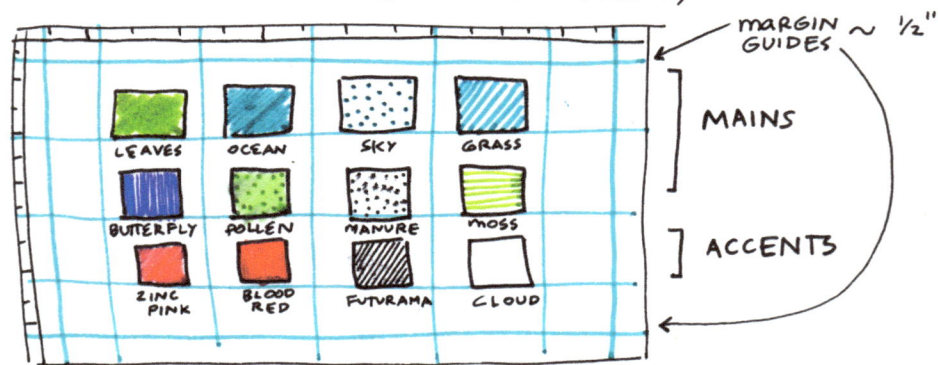

MARGIN GUIDES ~ ½"

MAINS

ACCENTS

LEAVES   OCEAN   SKY   GRASS

BUTTERFLY   POLLEN   MANURE   MOSS

ZINC PINK   BLOOD RED   FUTURAMA   CLOUD

A. CLICK ON ART BOARD USING MARQUIS TOOL
B. CHOOSE A COLOR FROM THE PALETTE
C. EDIT > FILL
      USE FOREGROUND COLOR
D. REPEAT A-C UNTIL YOU HAVE ALL 12 REPRESENTED

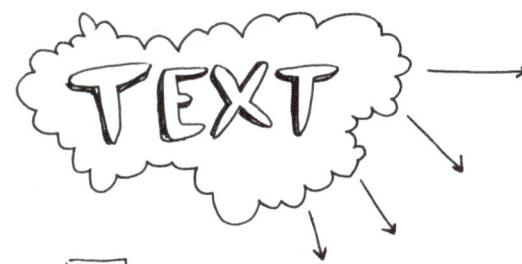

I THIS IS THE "TYPE TOOL"
CLICK ON IT IN THE TOOL BOX
CLICK ONCE ON THE ART BOARD

VS.

I THIS IS THE BLINKING "I" BAR = CLICK AND DRAG OVER AN EXISTING
PIECE OF TEXT TO MODIFY...

[I] THIS IS THE "I" BAR WITH A BOX AROUND IT = MAKE
A NEW PIECE OF TEXT

* MANY OPTIONS WITH TEXT

    I. FONT FAMILY (e.g. HELVETICA, TIMES, IMPACT, FUTURA)

    II. SIZE (IN POINTS)

    III. COLOR (CLICK THE 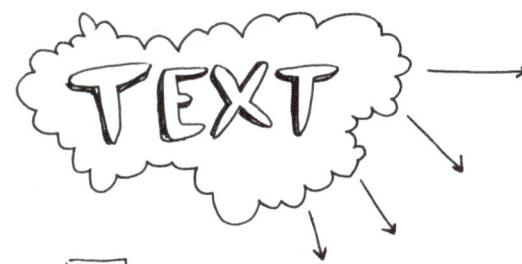 IN THE CONTROL PALETTE)
TO CHANGE COLOR...

    IV. TRACKING - THE ADJUSTMENT OF SPACE FOR GROUPS OF LETTERS

    V. KERNING - THE ADJUSTMENT OF SPACE BETWEEN PAIRS OF LETTERS

    VI. LEADING - THE SPACE BETWEEN LINES OF TEXT

    VII. BOLD, UNDERLINE, ITALICS, STRIKE THROUGH,
SMALL CAPS

* TO MAKE ADJUSTMENTS
OPEN THE CHARACTER PALETTE
WINDOW < CHARACTER
TO HIGHLIGHT THE TEXT, CLICK AND DRAG
WITH THE BOXED I BAR

E.G. YOU ARE BEAUTIFUL!

    HIGHLIGHTED, I CAN NOW ENLARGE
THE TEXT TO 60 pts AND MAKE
IT HOT PINK!

PATTERNS

PATTERNS IN PHOTOSHOP CONSIST OF 2 MAIN PARTS.

PART 1: GROUND

- EITHER A SQUARE OR A RECTANGLE
- THE GROUND HAS A SOLID FILL OR IN SOME INSTANCES A TEXTURAL PATTERN

PART 2: THE MOTIF(S)

- THESE ARE IMAGES RANGING FROM THE SIMPLEST TO THE MOST COMPLEX FORMS

* LET'S MAKE A POLKA DOT:

1) CREATE A 2" x 2" CANVAS
   FILE > NEW
   W = 2"
   H = 2"
   RESOLUTION = 300 P.P.I.
   COLOR MODE = RGB 8 BITS

2) THEN FILL THE CANVAS WITH 1 OF YOUR COLORS [GROUND]
   SELECT > ALL   (⌘A) SHORTCUT!
   EDIT > FILL → USE: FOREGROUND COLOR
   SELECT > DESELECT   (⌘D) SHORTCUT!

3) NEXT! PICK UP THE ELIPTICAL MARQUIS TOOL
   CLICK + DRAG OUT A SELECTION ON THE CANVAS
   *HINT! HOLD DOWN SHIFT TO CREATE A CIRCLE

4) FILL SELECTION ⬚ WITH COLOR   [MOTIF]
   EDIT < FILL → USE FOREGROUND COLOR
   1st PICK A COLOR FROM THE SWATCHES PALETTE
   THEN SELECT < DESELECT

5) 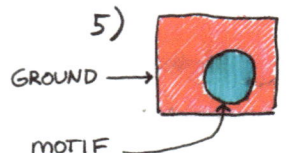 WHAT WE HAVE HERE IS A **REPEAT ELEMENT**
   GROUND →
   MOTIF →
   WHAT'S THAT? THIS IS A MODULE THAT TILES UP + DOWN <u>PLUS</u> BACK AND FORTH INFINITELY

6) NEXT... SELECT > ALL
   EDIT > DEFINE PATTERN
   NAME IT! POLKA DOT [OK] ✓

7) TO SEE THE FULL EFFECT
   FILE > NEW
   SIZE = 8.5" x 11" (LETTER SIZE)

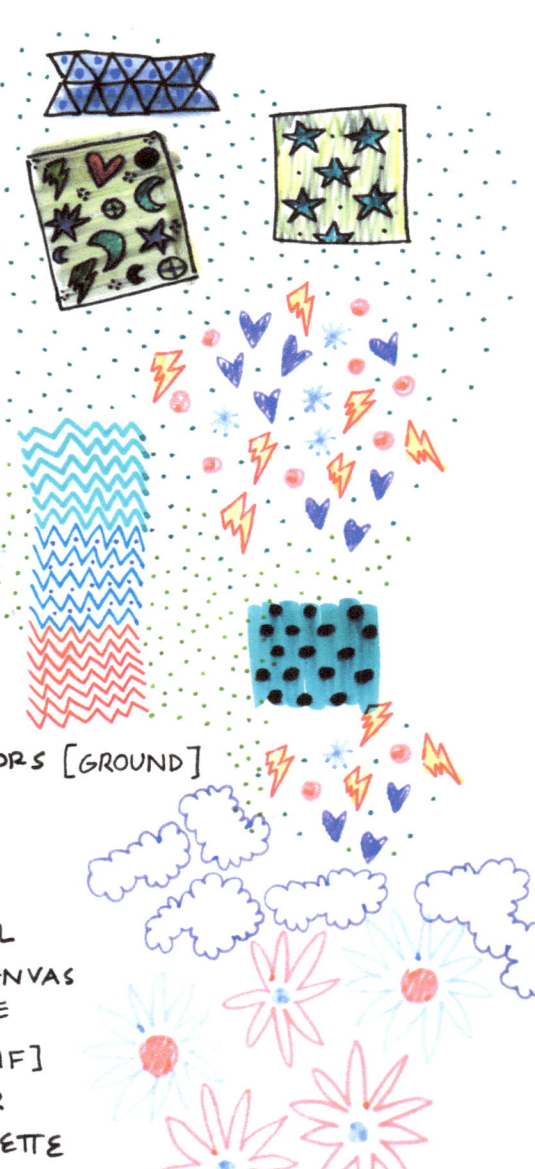

*★ PATTERNS *CONTINUED...

8) SELECT ENTIRE BLANK CANVAS
   SELECT > ALL

9) FILL WITH PATTERN
   EDIT > FILL
   USE: PATTERN
   SCROLL DOWN TO LAST SWATCH IN LIBRARY
   CLICK THE POLKA DOT [OK] ✓

10) WHAT YOU END UP IS THIS:

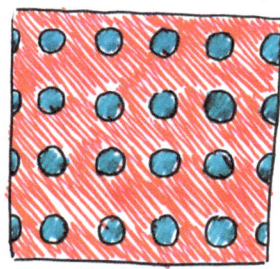 FROM THIS 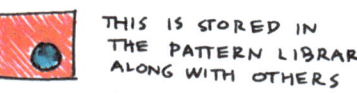 THIS IS STORED IN
THE PATTERN LIBRARY
ALONG WITH OTHERS

11) NAMING SYSTEM: POLKA DOT_LINK.TIF / POLKA DOT_RPT.TIF

   THE ELEMENT = _RPT
   THE LETTER SIZE PAGE = _LINK

SAVING YOUR WORK

I SAVE FILES AS EITHER .TIF OR .PSD EXTENSIONS
THESE ARE BOTH VERY HIGH QUALITY FILES

{SETTINGS} .TIF   ⊙ LZW COMPRESSION
                   (RETAINS THE INTEGRITY OF THE IMAGES)

         .PSD   USING LAYERS WILL INCREASE FILE SIZE
                 ☑ DON'T SHOW AGAIN   [OK] ⇐

         .JPG   ONLY USE WHEN SAVING WEB IMAGES
                 IMAGE > IMAGE SIZE
                 RESOLUTION = 72 PPI
                 FILE > SAVE
                 QUALITY = MAXIMUM
                 [OK] ⇐

✱ EXERCISE: CREATE THE FOLLOWING PATTERNS

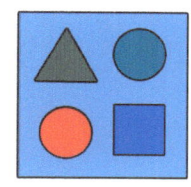 +

• USE 3"X3" SQUARES
  FOR THE GROUND
• USE A COMBINATION OF
  THE SELECTION TOOLS
  TO CREATE THE MOTIFS.

PATTERNS CONTINUED

MOTIFS (IMAGES)

IN PHOTOSHOP WE CAN GROUP IMAGES TO BE PREPARED FOR
TEXTILE DESIGNS INTO 2 CATEGORIES.
    THESE ARE: LINE ART (BLACK + WHITE IMAGES)
                   IMAGES IN COLOR (PAINTED MOTIFS, PHOTOS)

LET'S LOOK AT <u>LINE ART</u> FIRST...

ASSUMING THE ART IS SCANNED INTO PHOTOSHOP AT
300 PPI. OUR NEXT STEP IS:

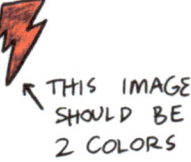

THE STARTING POINT... OUR IMAGE

USE THE PAINT BUCKET TO FILL WITH COLOR.

THIS IMAGE SHOULD BE 2 COLORS

1. IMAGE > ADJUSTMENTS > DESATURATE
    THIS SUCKS OUT THE SATURATION OF PIXELS
    MAKING THE IMAGE PURE GREYSCALE
    * NOTE! WE ARE STILL IN RGB MODE
      (IF YOU AREN'T, GO TO IMAGE > MODE > RGB)

2. NEXT... IMAGE > ADJUSTMENTS > THRESHOLD
    THIS GIVES US A PURE BLACK + WHITE IMAGE
    MOVE THE SLIDER RIGHT, BLACK OUTLINES THICKEN
    MOVE THE SLIDER LEFT, BLACK OUTLINES THIN OUT

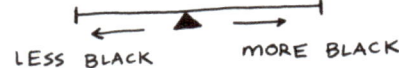

LESS BLACK   MORE BLACK

3. NOW WE ARE READY TO FILL THE IMAGE IN
    WITH COLOR. LET'S USE THE EXAMPLE OF A
    LIGHTNING BOLT ON A CANVAS OF 1" x 1".

4. PUT A COLOR YOU LIKE IN THE FOREGROUND →
    SWATCH FOUND IN THE TOOL BOX

5. CLICK THE PAINT BUCKET TOOL
    (THIS IS NESTED IN WITH THE GRADIENT- IT'S HIDING!)
    SETTINGS *   TOLERANCE [0]
              CONTIGUOUS ☑ (BECAUSE WE ONLY WANT
                             THE WHITE OF THE BOLT
                             TO CHANGE COLOR, NOT
                             THE BACKGROUND.)

6. CLICK ONCE IN THE CENTER
    OF THE IMAGE. VOILA!

  * TROUBLESHOOTING: IF YOU SEE AN OUTLINE OF GREY OR WHITE
        PIXELS ALONG THE EDGE BETWEEN THE RED + THE BLACK
        EDIT > UNDO, THEN RE-THRESHOLD (STEP # 2)

◎ SPEAKING OF EDIT > UNDO
    CAN WE EDIT > UNDO INDEFINITELY? NO. (ONLY IN ILLUSTRATOR) * HISTORY
                                                          PALETTE!
    IN PHOTOSHOP WE ARE LIMITED TO ABOUT 20 UNDOS
    THE GOOD NEWS IS ALL OF OUR FUNCTIONS PERFORMED
    CAN BE FOUND IN THE HISTORY PALETTE.
    WINDOW > HISTORY. CLICK BACK INTO THE PAST STATES
    TO UNDO COMMANDS.

MOTIFS   LINE ART! + LAYOUTS

NEXT LET'S CREATE A REPEAT LAYOUT USING A SINGLE LINE ART/BLACK + WHITE MOTIF.

1) DRAW A FLOWER, SCAN IT AT 300 D.P.I. AND LIKE OUR LIGHTNING BOLT IMAGE ON PG. 10, DESATURATE THEN THRESHOLD THE IMAGE. USE YOUR PAINT BUCKET TO FILL PETALS, LEAVES + CENTER WITH COLOR. FILE > SAVE AS... FLOWER_MOTIF.TIF

LINE ART

2) NEXT, CREATE A NEW FILE 5"x 5"

3) EDIT > FILL WITH A NICE BLUE

4) FILE > SAVE AS... FLOWER_RPT. TIF
⊙ LZW COMPRESSION [OK]

5) BACK TO THE MOTIF FILE... USE THE "LASSO" TOOL TO DRAW A SELECTION AROUND THE FLOWER

6) PICK UP THE "MAGIC WAND"
SETTINGS: TOLERANCE [0]
          CONTIGUOUS ☑
          ANTI-ALIAS ☐ UNCHECKED
HOLD DOWN OPTION/ALT KEY AND CLICK ONCE ON THE FLOWER'S BACKGROUND. THIS SUBTRACTS THE WHITE FROM THE SELECTION. WE NOW HAVE A PERFECT SELECTION SURROUNDING THE FLOWER.

7) USE THE MOVE TOOL ➤✛ TO MOVE THE FLOWER INTO THE RPT FILE (THE 5"x 5" SQUARE)

8) WHEN WE DROP AN IMAGE INTO A NEW CANVAS, A NEW LAYER IS CREATED AUTOMATICALLY. THE FLOWER IS HOUSED IN LAYER 1 THE SOLID BLUE IS HOUSED IN THE BACKGROUND

✱ HINT! DOUBLE CLICK THE BACKGROUND
CLICK [OK]
THIS UNLOCKS THE LAYER...

➤✛ MOVE TOOL SETTINGS:

☑ AUTO SELECT LAYER
THIS MAKES FINDING IMAGES EASIER ESPECIALLY WHEN WORKING W/MANY LAYERS.

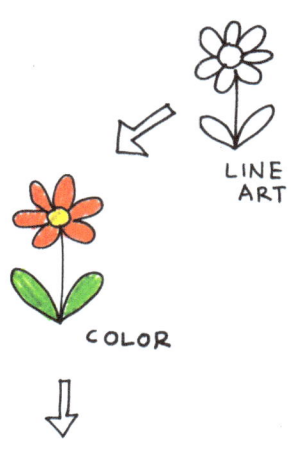
LINE ART

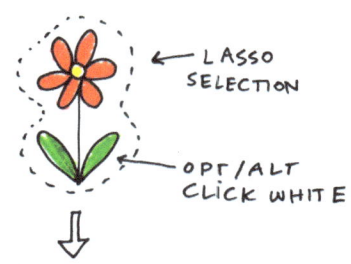
COLOR

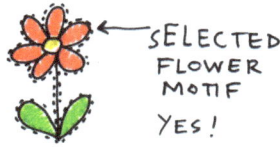
← LASSO SELECTION

← OPT/ALT CLICK WHITE

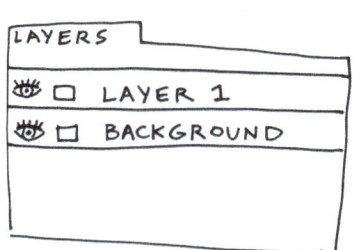
← SELECTED FLOWER MOTIF
YES!

LAYERS
👁 ☐ LAYER 1
👁 ☐ BACKGROUND

♥ WHAT ARE LAYERS?? THINK OF THEM AS PIECES OF CLEAR ACETATE OVER TOP OF 1 ANOTHER. SOME FILES HAVE AS MANY AS 200 LAYERS!

REPEAT LAYOUTS

WE NOW HAVE A FILE WITH A BACKGROUND + A FLOWER MOTIF
LET'S CONTINUE WITH THE LAYOUT...

1) FIRST DECIDE ON A LAYOUT BY CREATING A QUICK SKETCH
OF THE BASIC FLOW OF THE DESIGN... LIKE SO

♡ LAYOUT
    EXAMPLES ♡

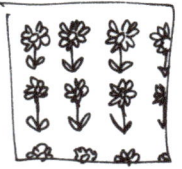
(1 WAY)
ONE-DIRECTIONAL

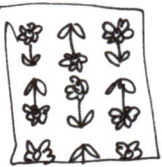
(2 WAY)
BI-DIRECTIONAL

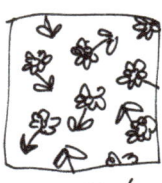
TOSSED/
ALLOVER

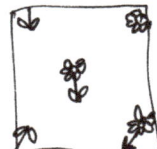
OPEN
(MORE
GROUND)

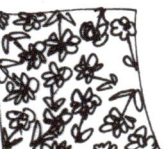
CLOSED
(LESS
GROUND)

2) HOW CAN WE MODIFY A MOTIF? WHAT TYPES OF CHANGES CAN WE MAKE?
- SCALE
- ROTATE
- COPY/PASTE
- MOVE
- REFLECT
- USE A FILTER
- USE IMAGE ADJUSTMENTS
- CHANGE THE COLOR(S)
- CLONE

3) INTRODUCING... FREE TRANSFORM
EDIT > FREE TRANSFORM OR ⌘ T
THE TRANSFORM BOX APPEARS
CLICK + DRAG TO SCALE UP OR DOWN
CONTROL CLICK (OR RIGHT CLICK PC)
    TO REFLECT, ROTATE, + OTHERS
* HINT! PRESS RETURN WHEN YOU ARE READY
    TO ACCEPT THE TRANSFORMATION

4) USING YOUR KNOWLEDGE OF TRANSFORM
CREATE 1 OF THE ABOVE LAYOUTS.
SAVE YOUR FILE.

5) LET'S DEFINE THE PATTERN + PLACE INTO
THE LIBRARY WITH EDIT > DEFINE PATTERN

6) CREATE A NEW LETTER SIZE PAGE

7) USE THE PAINT BUCKET TOOL
SETTINGS: USE
        CONTENTS = PATTERN
            SCROLL DOWN TO THE FLOWER_RPT SWATCH
    CLICK ONCE ON THE PAGE + VOILA!

INDEXED COLOR

WHERE DO MOTIFS IN COLOR COME FROM?
1. PHOTOS
2. DIGITAL PHOTOS
3. WEB IMAGES
4. PAINTED ARTWORK
5. COLLAGES
6. SCANNED IMAGES FROM A PICTURE COLLECTION

1) BEGIN BY DRAWING A MOTIF BY HAND IN COLOR
LET'S USE A RAINBOW.

2) SCAN IN AT 300 DPI

3) FILE > SAVE... RAINBOW_MOTIF.TIF

4) IMAGE > MODE > RGB

5) IMAGE > MODE > INDEXED COLOR
THIS WILL DEFINE THE COLORS FOR US
AND PLACE THEM IN A COLOR TABLE

FIGURE 1

DIALOG BOX #1   SETTINGS:

PALETTE: LOCAL
COLORS: [8]   (OUR RAINBOW HAS 8
                    COLORS. DON'T FORGET,
                    THE GROUND COUNTS!)

FORCED: CUSTOM

☐ PREVIEW
(UNCHECKED)

DIALOG BOX #2 = FORCED COLORS (COLOR TABLE)
HERE WE DEFINE THE COLORS

FORCED COLORS				
1	2	3	4	[OK]
5	6	7	8	[CANCEL]
				[LOAD]
				[SAVE]

• CLICK SQUARE 1 (UPPER LEFT)
• SHIFT CLICK CLICK
  THE YELLOW BAND IN THE
  RAINBOW [OK]
• CLICK →   IN THE
              COLOR PICKER

DIALOG BOX #3 = COLOR PICKER
THIS SHOWS UP WHEN YOU CLICK A SQUARE.
IGNORE IT FOR NOW- ONLY CHOOSE COLORS
IN YOUR DESIGN. WE WILL RE-COLOR LATER...
(FROM YOUR DESIGN)

* CONTINUE SELECTING COLORS IN THIS FASHION
  UNTIL ALL 8 COLORS ARE REPRESENTED

• CLICK [OK]   • IN DIALOG BOX #1 ☑ PREVIEW

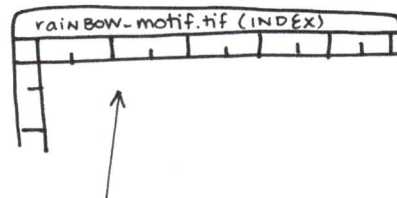

6) YOUR FILE IS NOW LABELED RAINBOW_MOTIF.TIF (INDEX)

CHANGING COLORS!

LET'S WORK WITH OUR FLOWER PATTERN + MAKE A
COLORWAY. WHAT'S THAT? A VERSION OF THE ORIGINAL
DESIGN IN DIFFERENT COLORS. WHETHER 1 COLOR CHANGES
OR THEY ALL DO, IT'S STILL A COLOR WAY (AKA: COLOR COMBO)

1) OPEN THE FILE FLOWER_RPT.TIF
   (OR GRAB from www.funkyjewels.com/flower_rpt.tif)

2) IMAGE > MODE > COLOR TABLE
   look familiar? this opens the dialog we used
   while indexing our rainbow motif.
   THERE WILL BE 6 COLORS IN THE COLOR TABLE

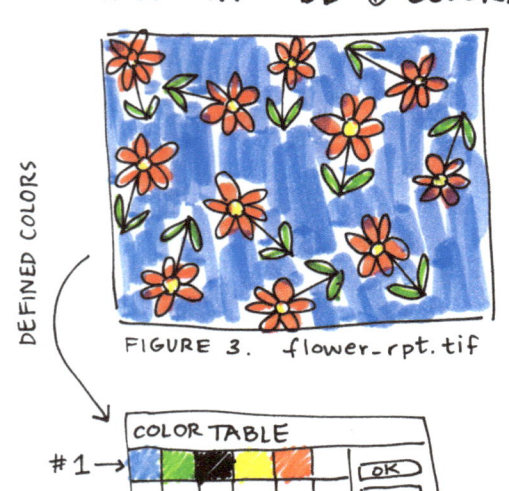

DEFINED COLORS

FIGURE 3. flower_rpt.tif

COLOR TABLE

#1 →

1. BLUE   3. BLACK   5. PINK
2. GREEN   4. YELLOW   6. WHITE

3) LET'S REPLACE COLORS IN THE
   TABLE WITH NEW ONES

   A. FROM THE COLOR PICKER
      · CHOOSE FROM THE RAINBOW
        BAR + VALUE/SATURATION FIELD
        (SEE PAGE 5)

   B. FROM SWATCHES PALETTE
      · OPEN COLOR STORY
      · CLICK ONCE ON SQUARE #1
      · CHOOSE A COLOR FROM
        YOUR PALETTE.
      · CONTINUE IN THIS FASHION
        UNTIL ALL COLORS ARE REPLACED
      · THEN CLICK [OK]

      * HINT! THE PALETTE MUST BE OPEN
        BEFORE OPENING THE
        COLOR TABLE.

4) SAVE FILE AS FLOWER_RPTA.TIF
   FOR SUBSEQUENT COLORWAYS, LABEL RPT B, RPTC, ETC.

* TROUBLESHOOTING:
   WHAT IF MY TABLE HAS AN EXTRA COLOR IN IT, SAY A
   RED THAT DOESN'T BELONG?
   NO PROBLEM! SIMPLY RE-INDEX ⟹ IMAGE > MODE > RGB
                                  IMAGE > MODE > INDEXED COLOR
                                  CHOOSE THE CORRECT COLORS

HALF DROPS

WHAT'S A ½ DROP?

1st Let's DEFINE A SQUARE REPEAT:

IF WE HAVE A REPEAT
MODULE LIKE THIS:
WE CALL IT SQUARE.
THE LAYOUT IT YIELDS
IS THIS:

SQUARE
REPEAT

SQUARE
LAYOUT.

OK. SO A ½ DROP   USING THE
SAME MOTIF LOOKS LIKE THIS:
THE LAYOUT IT YIELDS
IS THIS:

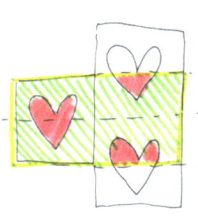

HALF
DROP
REPEAT

½ DROP
LAYOUT

[THE MOTIFS
FORM A
DIAMOND LIKE
LAYOUT]

HOW DO WE MAKE ONE?

1) START W/ 3×3" CANVAS. (L= GREEN)

2) CREATE A NICE PINK ♡ IN THE CENTER

3) MAKE GUIDES
    5

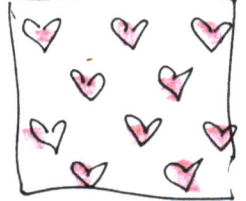

VIEW < SNAP
← CENTER

4) SELECT > ALL
   EDIT > COPY.

5) IMAGE > CANVAS SIZE

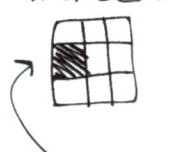

CLICK ANCHOR

TOGGLE INCHES → PERCENT
HEIGHT = 100 %
WIDTH = 200 %

OK √

HALF DROPS

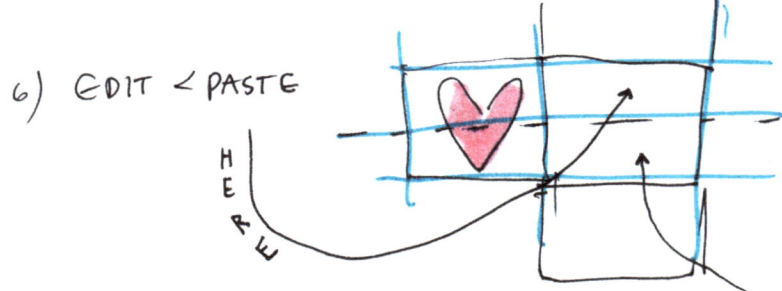

6) EDIT < PASTE

**H
E
R
E**

7) SNAP IN PLACE (UPPER RT) <u>BASE</u> OF
♡ LINES UP W/ <u>CENTER</u> GUIDE.

8) EDIT > PASTE AGAIN!
THIS TIME HERE ___ (LOWER RT)
<u>TOP</u> OF ♡ LINES UP W/ CENTER GUIDE.

9) LAYER > FLATTEN IMAGE
↳ VOILA →

(0) EDIT > DEFINE PATTERN
NAME IT HEART_HALF DROP!

11) LET'S SEE THIS THING TILE...

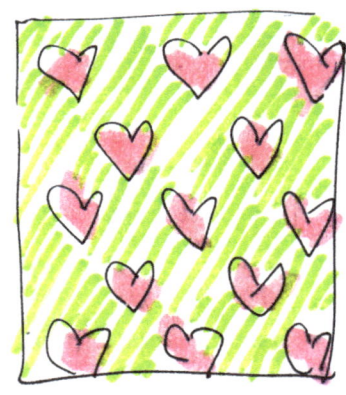

· FILE > NEW (LETTER SIZE)
· EDIT > FILL
USE: PATTERN
CHOOSE ♡ HALF DROP
· THIS IS OUR RESULT

COMPLEX LAYOUTS (OFFSET!)

AT TIMES WE WILL NEED TO OFFSET A REPEAT MODULE TO MAKE ADJUSTMENTS WITHIN A LAYOUT. WE WILL USE THE FILTER → FILTER > OTHER > OFFSET FOR THIS PURPOSE.

(1) FIG.

(2) FIG.

(3) FIG.   RESULT!

1) LET'S BEGIN BY CREATING A NEW 3"x3" FILE.

2) FILL THE BACKGROUND WITH GREEN

3) DRAW A STAR USING THE POLYGON LASSO TOOL AND FILL WITH COLOR

4) CREATE THE HEART W/ THE LASSO. FILL W/COLOR.

5) CREATE THE ½ CIRCLE USING THE ELIPTICAL MARQUIS. FILL W/COLOR

6) GO TO FILTER > OTHER > OFFSET
   SETTINGS: ⊙ WRAP AROUND
             ☑ PREVIEW
   MOVE THE SLIDERS UNTIL THE MODULE LOOKS LIKE FIG. (2). [OK] ⇦

7) WE HAVE 2 IMAGES TO CORRECT/MAKE WHOLE. USE THE PENCIL TO FILL IN THE BLANKS, TO MAKE A STAR, A HEART + A CIRCLE. FIG (3)

8) EDIT > DEFINE PATTERN
   NAME IT + CHOOSE OK!

9) FILE > SAVE AS... TRIO-RPT. TIF

10) LET'S SEE IT TILE ON A LETTER SIZE PAGE. FILE > NEW > LETTER SIZE.
    EDIT > FILL > USE PATTERN <
    FIND IT ! [OK] ⇐

✱ INTRODUCING: OUTLINES!
  · USE THE WAND TO SELECT THE HEART
       TOLERANCE = [1]
            ☐ ANTI ALIAS , ☐ CONTIGUOUS (UNCHECK)
  · LAYER > CREATE A NEW LAYER
  · ƒx = STYLE LAYER BUTTON · CLICK IT, CHOOSE STROKE
       THEN CHANGE COLOR, PIXEL SIZE, + MORE IN
       THE SETTING.
  · REPEAT WITH THE CIRCLE + THE STAR

THE WORLD OF PLAIDS + STRIPES

☆ STRIPES ☆

WE CAN CREATE STRIPES FAIRLY EASILY WITH THE
HELP OF THE MARQUIS TOOL. STRIPES ARE PATTERNS, SO
WHEN WE ARE DESIGNING, LET'S KEEP IN MIND THE
SMALLEST ELEMENT THAT WILL REPEAT. FOR EXAMPLE:

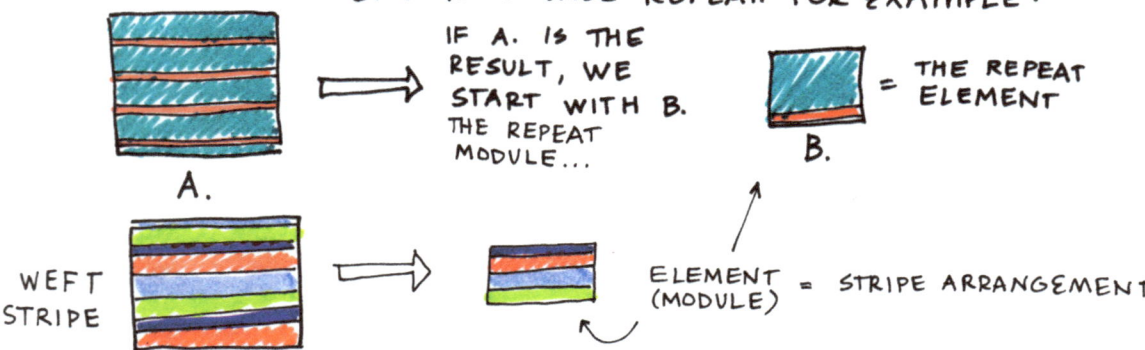

A.

IF A. IS THE
RESULT, WE
START WITH B.
THE REPEAT
MODULE...

= THE REPEAT
ELEMENT

B.

WEFT
STRIPE

ELEMENT
(MODULE) = STRIPE ARRANGEMENT

1) FILE > NEW
   DIMENSIONS = 3" X 3"
   RGB 8 BIT , 300 P.P.I.

2) WINDOW > SWATCHES
   DROP DOWN MENU > REPLACE SWATCHES
   (LOAD YOUR COLOR STORY FROM PAGE 6)

3) PICK UP THE RECTANGULAR MARQUIS TOOL
   CLICK + DRAG AN AREA THAT REPRESENTS
   1 STRIPE IN THE ARRANGEMENT.

4) PICK A COLOR FROM THE PALETTE
   USE FOREGROUND COLOR   [OK]
   EDIT > FILL

5) CONTINUE TO REPEAT STEPS
   3 + 4 UNTIL YOUR ARRANGEMENT IS COMPLETE.

6) NOW LET'S DEFINE THE PATTERN
   EDIT > DEFINE PATTERN
   NAME IT! VERTICAL STRIPE

7) TO SEE THE PATTERN TILE,
   FILE > NEW ... LETTER SIZE PAGE

8) EDIT > FILL
   USE PATTERN, SCROLL DOWN TO
   YOUR WARP STRIPE PATTERN
   THUMBNAIL... SUCCESS!

SELECTION FOR
1 STRIPE

3 X 3" CANVAS

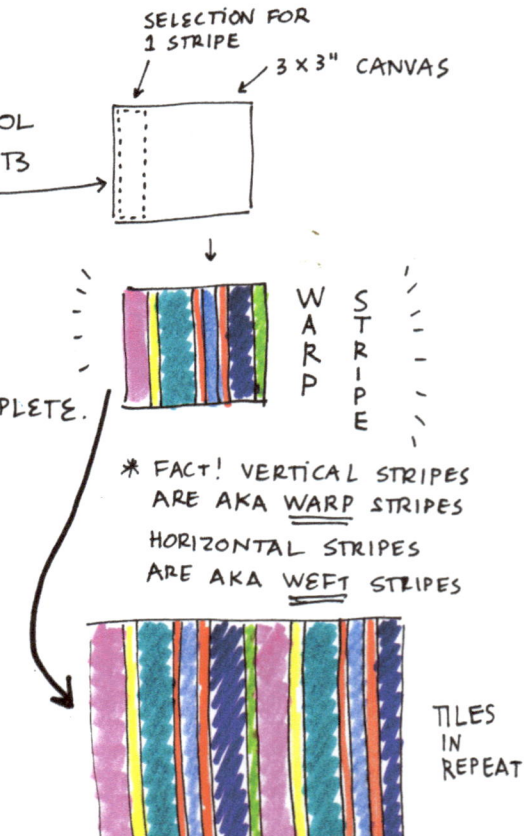

WARP STRIPE

☀ FACT! VERTICAL STRIPES
ARE AKA WARP STRIPES

HORIZONTAL STRIPES
ARE AKA WEFT STRIPES

TILES
IN
REPEAT ♥

PLAIDS

⊙ WHAT IS A PLAID?
PLAIDS ARE CREATED WHEN THE YARNS IN BOTH THE WARP
AND WEFT CONTAIN ALTERNATING BANDS OF COLOR.

✳ THE WEAVER'S
LOOM HOLDS THE
WARP YARNS IN
PLACE WHILE THE
WEFT YARNS ARE
WOVEN THROUGH.

LET'S CREATE A PLAID THAT USES A TRADITIONAL
TARTAN AS INSPIRATION.
WE WILL BE CREATING A WARP STRIPE + A WEFT STRIPE
                    (VERTICAL)   (HORIZONTAL)

1) FILE > NEW
   SIZE: 3" x 3"

2) FOLLOWING STEPS FROM PAGE 18, CREATE THE FOLLOWING:

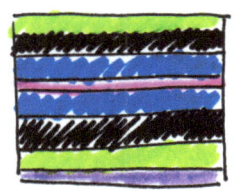
WARP

   • SELECT > ALL
   • EDIT > DEFINE PATTERN
     ✳ NAME IT: TARTAN WARP
   • SAVE FILE, FILE < SAVE AS... TARTAN WARP TIF

3) NEXT, LET'S TURN THE VERTICAL STRIPE BY ROTATING 90°

   IMAGE > ROTATE CANVAS > 90° CLOCKWISE
   VOILA! WE NOW HAVE OUR WEFT STRIPE.
   EDIT > DEFINE PATTERN (NAME IT TARTAN WEFT)
   FILE > SAVE AS > TARTANWEFT. TIF

WEFT

✳ THE WARP + WEFT ARE
WOVEN AT RIGHT ANGLES
TO EACH OTHER.

4) LET'S COMBINE THEM... FILE < NEW (SIZE = LETTER)
   RE-INTRODUCING THE LAYERS PALETTE HERE.
   WE WILL MAKE 2 LAYERS.
   LAYER 1 = WARP   OPACITY = 100%.
   LAYER 2 = WEFT   OPACITY = 50%.

✳✳✳✳
GET IT? THE TRANSPARENCY
OF THE WEFT ALLOWS THE
WARP TO SHINE THROUGH A BIT!

5) EDIT > FILL, USE PATTERN = WARP

6) IN THE LAYERS PALETTE → DROP DOWN MENU
   ADD NEW LAYER (CREATE)
   EDIT > FILL, USE PATTERN = WEFT

7) CHANGE OPACITY IN THE LAYERS
   PALETTE. = 50%

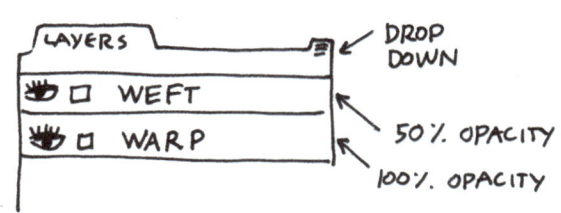
LAYERS
👁 ☐ WEFT
👁 ☐ WARP
→ DROP DOWN
← 50% OPACITY
← 100% OPACITY

✳ FUN FACT! PLAID COMES
FROM A GAELIC
WORD MEANING BLANKET

WEAVES

WE AREN'T TALKING ABOUT HAIR WEAVES HERE! BUT THE MANNER IN WHICH THE WARP + FILL THREADS INTERLACE WITH ONE ANOTHER IN A WOVEN FABRIC.

PLAIN WEAVE

FIG. 5

THE PLAIN WEAVE IS THE SIMPLEST WOVEN STRUCTURE WHERE FILL THREADS ALTERNATE UNDER, OVER, UNDER, OVER WARP THREADS.

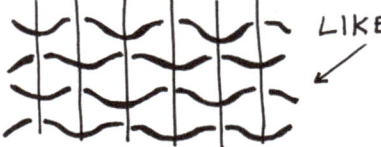

LIKE SO... WE WILL REPRESENT IT IN PHOTOSHOP AS FIGURE 5.

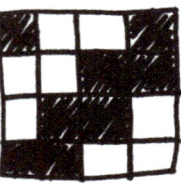

2x2 TWILL

BASKET WEAVE

← OTHER WELL KNOWN WEAVES. MAKE UP YOUR OWN COMPLEX WEAVES AND SEE OELSNER'S HANDBOOK OF WEAVES IN THE BIBLIOGRAPHY SECTION.

LET'S BEGIN WITH THE PLAIN WEAVE

1) FILE > NEW   SIZE = 1" x 1"

2) USE THE FIXED SIZE SETTING OF THE RECTANGULAR MARQUIS TOOL TO CREATE 2 SQUARES USING BLACK AS THE FOREGROUND. LIKE SO: 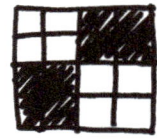 . FEEL FREE TO CREATE GUIDES TO PLACE SQUARES DIAGONALLY ACROSS FROM EACH OTHER.

3) USE THE NORMAL SETTING FOR THE RECTANGULAR MARQUIS TO CREATE A SELECTION AROUND THE CHECKER-BOARD. = REPEAT ELEMENT

4) IMAGE > CROP

5) LAYERS > FLATTEN IMAGE

6) EDIT > DEFINE PATTERN

7) NAME PATTERN "PLAIN WEAVE"

8) FILE > SAVE AS... PLAIN WEAVE.TIF

NOW LET'S FILL A PAGE WITH THE WEAVE...

9) FILE > NEW   SIZE = LETTER

10) EDIT > FILL
USE PATTERN ▼
CHOOSE PLAIN WEAVE THUMBNAIL OK ←

11) FILE > SAVE AS...
PLAIN WEAVE_TEMPLATE.TIF

✱ INTRODUCING: SNAP! SNAP TO GUIDES WILL MAKE OBJECTS AND VARIOUS SELECTIONS FEEL MAGNETICALLY ATTRACTED TO ANY GUIDES ON THE ARTBOARD. FEEL THE PULL!!

PLAIDS + WEAVES

LET'S COMBINE THESE 2 ELEMENTS TO YIELD A SIMULATED PIECE OF CLOTH.

1) FIRST, LET'S OPEN PLAIN WEAVE_TEMPLATE.TIF ON THIS PAGE, THE BLACK SQUARES REPRESENT THE WARP + THE WHITE SQUARES REPRESENT THE WEFT (AKA FILL).

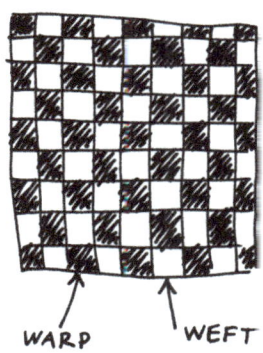

WARP   WEFT

2) KNOWING THIS, LET'S MAKE SURE THE PATTERNS TARTAN WARP AND TARTAN WEFT ARE BOTH HOUSED IN THE PATTERN LIBRARY FROM PAGE 19. DO A CHECK WITH EDIT > FILL, USE PATTERN, SCROLL DOWN AND LOOK FOR THE THUMBNAILS.

3) NEXT WE WILL SELECT ALL OF THE BLACK SQUARES USING THE WAND. PICK UP THE MAGIC WAND.
SETTINGS: TOLERANCE [1]
ANTI-ALIAS ☐ } NOT
CONTIGUOUS ☐ } CHECKED

4) CLICK ONCE ON A BLACK SQUARE. ALL BLACK SQUARES ARE SELECTED

5) NEXT WE'LL FILL THE AREA WITH THE WARP PATTERN. EDIT > FILL
USE PATTERN, SCROLL TO TARTAN WARP
[OK] ⇐

* INTRODUCING... SELECT < INVERSE AFTER FINISHING STEP 5, WE CAN GO TO SELECT < INVERSE. THIS WILL AUTOMATICALLY SELECT ALL PREVIOUSLY DESELECTED PIXELS. IN OUR CASE THE DESELECTED PIXELS ARE THE WHITE ONES.

6) SELECT > DESELECT (⌘D)

7) REPEAT STEPS 3-5, BUT THIS TIME WE ARE SELECTING A WHITE SQUARE/ ALL WHITE AREAS + FILLING THE SELECTION WITH THE WEFT STRIPE ARRANGEMENT

8) SELECT > DESELECT

9) ZOOM OUT (⌘-) TO VIEW YOUR PLAID IN ALL OF ITS WONDER...

b) FILE > SAVE AS... TARTAN PLAID.TIF

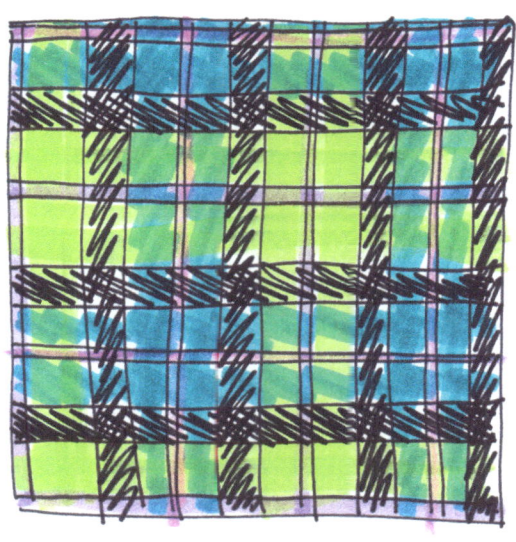

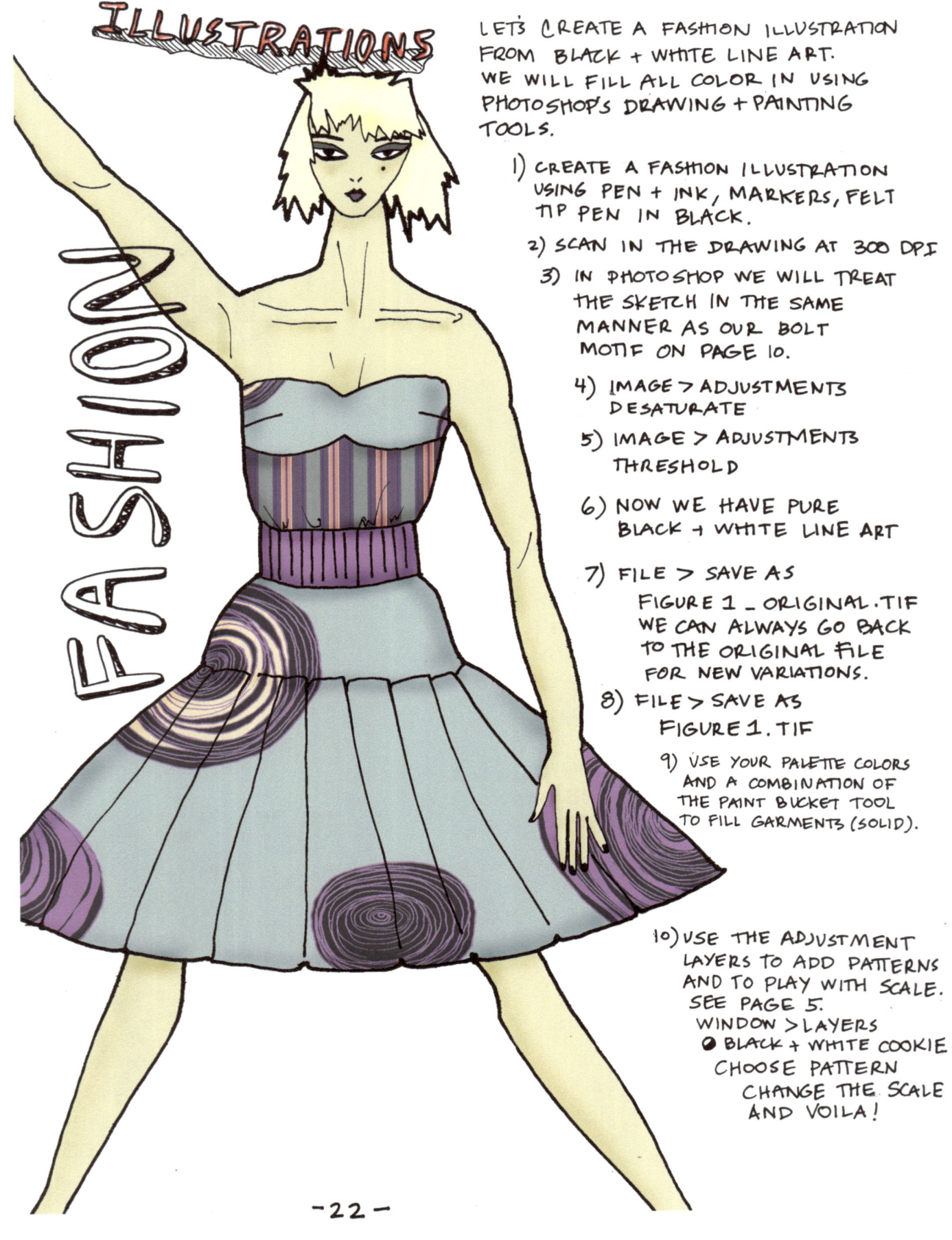

ILLUSTRATIONS

FASHION

LET'S CREATE A FASHION ILLUSTRATION FROM BLACK + WHITE LINE ART. WE WILL FILL ALL COLOR IN USING PHOTOSHOP'S DRAWING + PAINTING TOOLS.

1) CREATE A FASHION ILLUSTRATION USING PEN + INK, MARKERS, FELT TIP PEN IN BLACK.

2) SCAN IN THE DRAWING AT 300 DPI

3) IN PHOTOSHOP WE WILL TREAT THE SKETCH IN THE SAME MANNER AS OUR BOLT MOTIF ON PAGE 10.

4) IMAGE > ADJUSTMENTS DESATURATE

5) IMAGE > ADJUSTMENTS THRESHOLD

6) NOW WE HAVE PURE BLACK + WHITE LINE ART

7) FILE > SAVE AS
FIGURE 1 _ ORIGINAL . TIF
WE CAN ALWAYS GO BACK TO THE ORIGINAL FILE FOR NEW VARIATIONS.

8) FILE > SAVE AS
FIGURE 1 . TIF

9) USE YOUR PALETTE COLORS AND A COMBINATION OF THE PAINT BUCKET TOOL TO FILL GARMENTS (SOLID).

10) USE THE ADJUSTMENT LAYERS TO ADD PATTERNS AND TO PLAY WITH SCALE. SEE PAGE 5.
WINDOW > LAYERS
● BLACK + WHITE COOKIE
CHOOSE PATTERN
CHANGE THE SCALE AND VOILA!

FASHION ILLUSTRATIONS CONTINUED

WE HAVE OUR BASIC FIGURE FILLED WITH PATTERN AND COLOR SITTING ON A WHITE BACKGROUND. NOW LET'S ADD IN SOME DETAILS LIKE SHADOWS, HIGHLIGHTS, AND DROP SHADOWS.

I. THE DROP SHADOW
THE DROP SHADOW WILL BE CREATED BY MAKING A SELECTION AROUND THE SILHOUETTE OF THE FIGURE, FILLING IT WITH A SOLID + THEN GIVING IT A BIT OF A BLUR + ANGLING IT SLIGHTLY DEPENDING ON THE LIGHT SOURCE.

1) **FLATTEN THE IMAGE**
   LAYER > FLATTEN IMAGE

2) **MAKE THE SELECTION**
   USE THE MAGIC WAND TOOL
   WITH SETTINGS : TOLERANCE = 1
                  ANTI-ALIAS ☐ UNCHECK
                  CONTIGUOUS ☑
   CLICK ONCE ON THE WHITE BACKGROUND
   IF THERE ARE BITS MISSING LIKE BETWEEN
   ARM + WAIST OR HAND AND LEG
   USE YOUR SHIFT KEY + CLICK,
   TO ADD IN THE PIECES TO YOUR SELECTION.
   NOW WE HAVE THE INVERSE SELECTED.

3) **SELECT THE INVERSE**
   SELECT > INVERSE

4) **MAKE A NEW LAYER**
   LAYER > ADD NEW LAYER

5) **EDIT > FILL**
   USE FOREGROUND COLOR
   (ONE OF YOUR CHOICE)

6) **BLUR IT!**
   FILTER > BLUR > GAUSSIAN BLUR
   ADJUST SLIDER AS NEEDED

7) **FILE > SAVE**

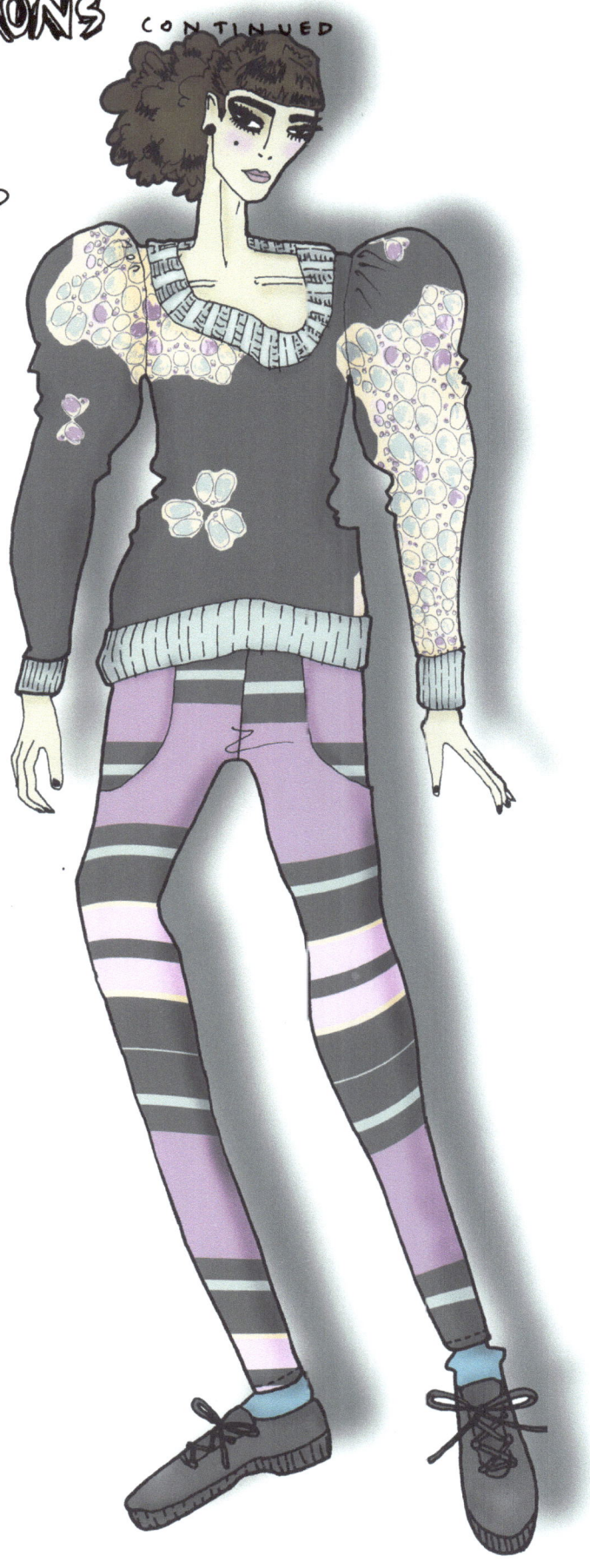

ILLUSTRATIONS

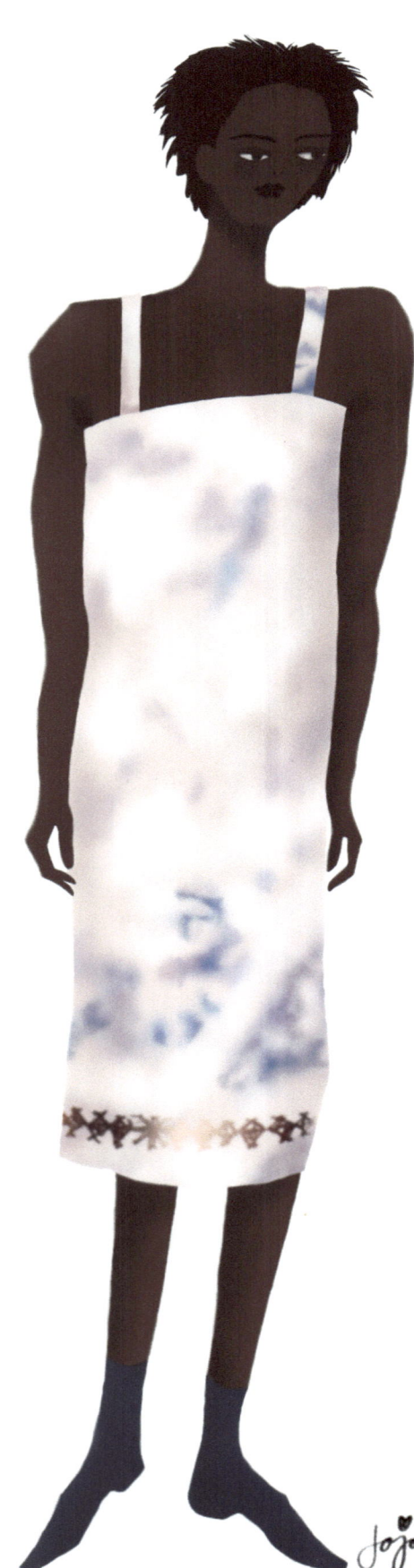

II. SHADOWS + HIGHLIGHTS

1. 1st MAKE A SELECTION AROUND THE GARMENT USING THE MAGIC WAND. <u>SETTINGS:</u>
   TOLERANCE ☐1☐   CONTIGUOUS ☑
   ANTI-ALIAS ☐   (THEN ADD TO SELECTION AS NECESSARY)

2. USE THE BURN TOOL TO SOFTLY SPRAY IN SOME SHADOWS.
   USE THE DODGE TOOL TO ADD HIGHLIGHTS.

3. LAYER THE AIRBRUSHING AND REMOVE ANY EXCESS WITH THE ERASER.
   <u>SETTING</u>S: BRUSH / SOFT
   OPACITY ⌵ 50%
   FLOW ⌵ 30%

4. ALTERNATE USING BRUSH + ERASER UNTIL YOU ACHEIVE YOUR DESIRED RESULT. * HINT! HAVE A PHOTO NEXT TO YOU THAT WILL SERVE AS A REFERENCE FOR SHADING, HIGHLIGHTS AND VOLUME OF THE FIGURE. PLUS - KEEP IN MIND... WHERE IS THE LIGHT SOURCE COMING FROM? UPPER RIGHT, LEFT ? ETC...

III. BACKGROUNDS
USE THE IMAGE SEARCH ENGINES ON THE INTERNET OR PICTURE COLLECTIONS AT THE LIBRARY TO FIND INTERESTING LANDSCAPES AND INTERIORS TO HOUSE YOUR FASHION ILLUSTRATIONS.
1. ADD A NEW LAYER.
2. OPEN THE IMAGE (BACKGROUND).
3. DRAG + DROP WITH THE MOVE TOOL INTO THE EXISTING FILE.

Flat Sketching

LET'S CREATE SOME FLAT GARMENT SKETCHES BASED ON OUR EARLIER FASHION ILLUSTRATIONS.

1) USE THE CROQUIS FIGURE IN THE APPENDIX [SEE PG. VI] TO DRAW THE GARMENT USING TRACING PAPER.

2) SCAN THE IMAGE(S) AT 300 DPI.

3) WE ARE WORKING WITH LINE ART HERE SO... WE WILL 1st DESATURATE + THRESHOLD AS IN PAGE 22.

4) LET'S CREATE AN 11x17" LAYOUT (LANDSCAPE) FILE > NEW / H = 11 , W = 17 / 300 DPI RGB , 8 BIT COLOR.

5) USE THE LASSO TOOL TO CREATE A SELECTION AROUND EACH IMAGE AND DRAG THEM INTO THE 17 x 11" PAGE ONE BY ONE USING THE MOVE TOOL. FILE > SAVE AS... FLAT3.TIF

6) ZOOM IN TO CHECK YOURSELF, SEE THAT YOU HAVE ONLY BLACK PIXELS ON A WHITE CANVAS. IF YOU SEE ANY GREY PIXELS, RE-THRESHOLD THE FILE.

7) USE A COMBINATION OF THE PAINT BUCKET TOOL + YOUR SWATCHES TO FILL ALL PATTERN PIECES WITH SOLIDS AND PATTERNS.

8) SEE PG. 22 TO EXPERIMENT WITH THE ⬤ ICON AS AN ALTERNATIVE.

FLATS:
IMAGE > ADJUSTMENT3 THRESHOLD

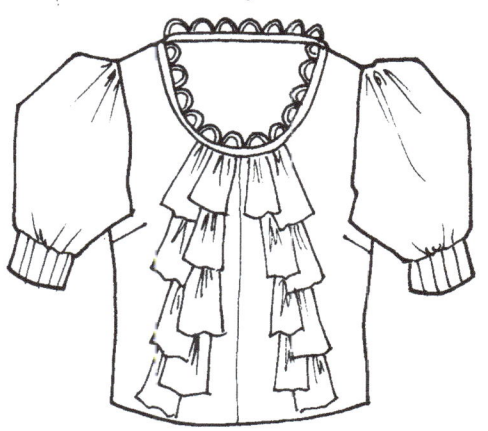

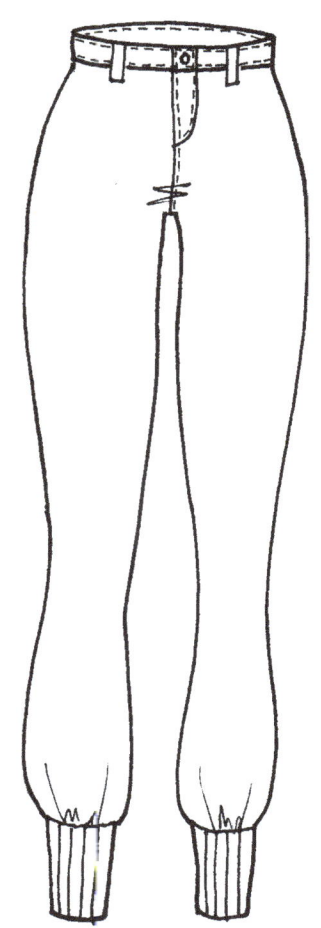

FLATS:
IMAGE >
ADJUSTMENT3 >
LEVELS

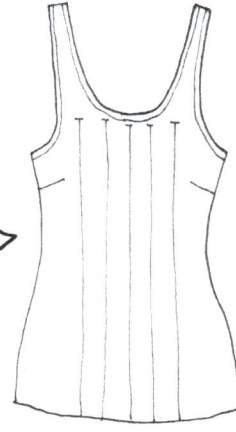

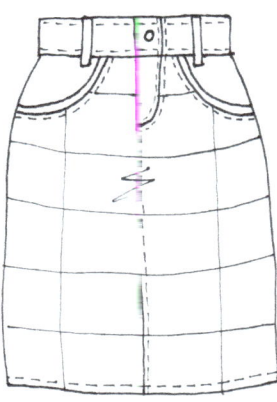

-25-

APPENDIX

SCANNING

"KEEP IT IN MIND"

PHOTOSHOP SHORTCUTS

TEXTILE DESIGN GLOSSARY

PRINTING

FEMALE CROQUIS *figure*

MALE CROQUIS *figure*

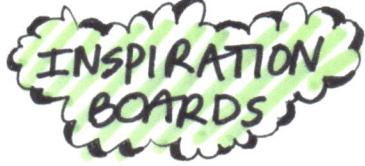
INSPIRATION BOARDS

BIBLIOGRAPHY

SCANNING + IMPORTING IMAGES

1. PLACE IMAGE ON SCANNER BED
2. OPEN PHOTOSHOP
3. FILE > IMPORT > CHOOSE SCANNER NAME
4. PREVIEW THE SCAN
5. <u>SETTINGS</u>:   FULL COLOR OR PHOTOGRAPH MODE
             300 D.P.I.
6. CHOOSE SCAN
7. THE SCANNED IMAGE OPENS IN PHOTOSHOP
8. CHECK TO MAKE SURE THE COLOR MODE IS RGB
9. SAVE FILE. FILE > SAVE AS
10. TYPE FILE NAME
     CHOOSE .TIF FILE EXTENSION
     USE LZW COMPRESSION
     CLICK SAVE

✳ HINT!
300 IS THE
MAGIC #
WHEN SCANNING!

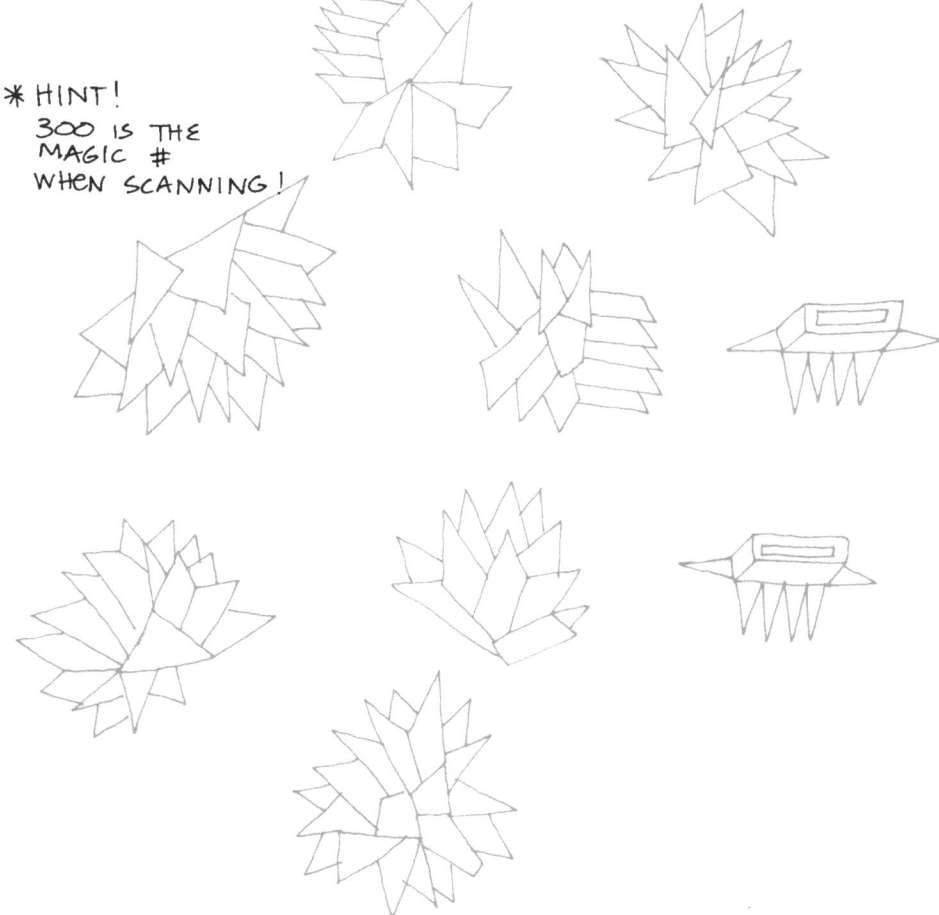

"KEEP IT IN MIND"

HERE ARE A FEW THINGS TO KEEP IN MIND WHEN WORKING WITH RASTERS.

1) ALWAYS SCAN IMAGES AT 300 D.P.I. CHECK YOURSELF USING IMAGE< IMAGE SIZE

2) SET IT UP, PREPARE BEFORE USING A TOOL FROM THE TOOL CHEST THE CONTROL PALETTE Ⓑ WILL CHANGE DEPENDING ON THE TOOL SELECTED

3) SELECTION TOOLS ARE WONDERFUL, BUT THEY WILL NOT MOVE PIXELS CONTAINED IN A SELECTION. IF YOU TRY TO DO THIS, THE MARCHING ANTS MOVE, THE PIXELS STAY PUT. TRY USING THE <u>MOVE TOOL</u> TO MOVE PIXELS CONTAINED IN A SELECTION.

THE INTERFACE + ITS PARTS:

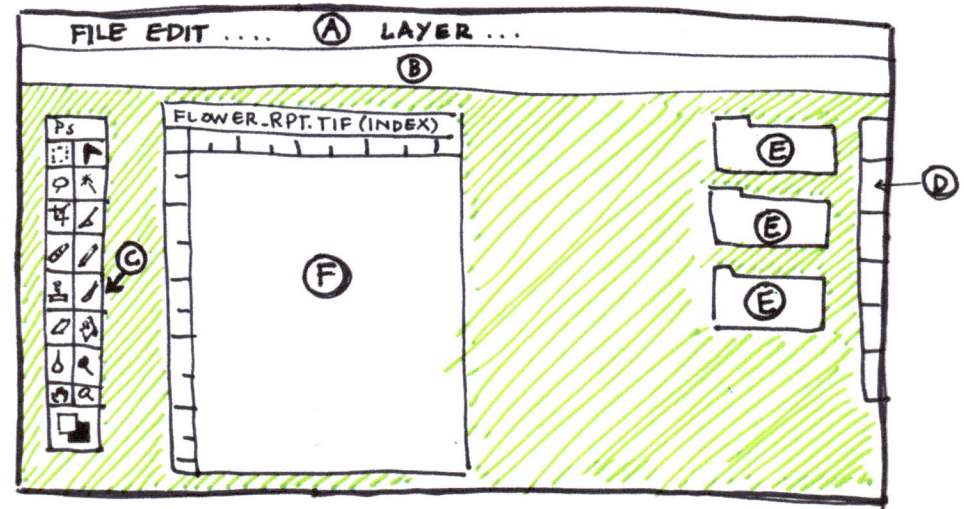

Ⓐ MENU BAR

Ⓑ CONTROL PALETTE

Ⓒ TOOL BOX
TOOL KIT
TOOL CHEST

Ⓓ PALETTE ICONS

Ⓔ PALETTES
(HISTORY, LAYERS, SWATCHES, ETC.)

Ⓕ CANVAS
FILE
WINDOW
ARTBOARD

PHOTOSHOP SHORTCUTS ♡ ☆ ⚡ ✳ ♡ ☆ ⚡ ✳ ♡

MAC + PC DIFFERENCES:

COMMAND ⌘ = CONTROL (CTRL)   ⇧ = SHIFT ICON
OPTION = ALT
CONTROL CLICK = RIGHT CLICK

MAC		P.C.	
⌘ P	PRINT	SPACE BAR	HAND TOOL
⌘ S	SAVE	ALT (OPT)	USED IN CONJUNCTION WITH THE MOVE TOOL WILL COPY THE ACTIVE SELECTION + MOVE IT
⌘ O	OPEN		
⌘ W	CLOSE WINDOW		
⌘ Q	CLOSE PROGRAM	⌘ R	RULERS
⌘ Z	UNDO/REDO TOGGLE	⌘ BACKSPACE	BACKGROUND COLOR ⎤ EDIT<
⌘ X	CUT	ALT-BACKSPACE	FOREGROUND COLOR ⎦ FILL WITH
⌘ C	COPY	ALT ⌘ I	IMAGE< IMAGE SIZE
⌘ V	PASTE	F12	REVERT
⌘ A	SELECT <-ALL	F7	WINDOW < LAYERS
⌘ D	SELECT < DESELECT		
⌘ +	ZOOM IN	S	CLONE STAMP
⌘ −	ZOOM OUT	D	DEFAULT FOREGROUND/ BACKGROUND
⌘ Ø	FIT IN WINDOW	G	GRADIENT
⌘ I	ACTUAL SIZE	T	TYPE TOOL
⌘ T	FREE TRANSFORM	C	CROP TOOL
OPT ⌘ Z	STEP BACKWARD	E	ERASER TOOL
OPT ⌘ C	CANVAS SIZE	P	PEN TOOL
⌘ F	LAST FILTER	W	MAGIC WAND
⇧⌘ I	SELECT < INVERSE	B	BRUSH TOOL
⌘ E	MERGE LAYERS	I	EYE DROPPER
		L	LASSO
		V	MOVE TOOL
		M	MARQUIS TOOL

SELECTIONS

☐ NEW

◪ ADD TO

▨ SUBTRACT

▧ INTERSECT

TEXTILE DESIGN GLOSSARY

ABSTRACT - IMAGES THAT HAVE BEEN STYLIZED EMPHASIZING LINES, COLORS, AND GENERALIZED/GEOMETRIC FORMS.

ALLOVER- A LAYOUT WHERE MULTIPLE FORMS OF A MOTIF(S) ARE ROTATED AND REFLECTED IN DIFFERENT WAYS + ARE DISTRIBUTED IN A BALANCED WAY.

BALANCED DESIGN- A DESIGN THAT HAS NO OBVIOUS SPACES, GAPS OR LINES FORMED BY THE DISTRIBUTION OF MOTIFS. NOR DOES ONE MOTIF ASSERT ITSELF OVER THE OTHERS.

BLOCK PRINTING- THE DESIGN IS CARVED ONTO WOOD BLOCKS. EACH COLOR HAS ITS OWN BLOCK. ITS ONE OF THE EARLIEST FORMS OF TEXTILE PRINTING. THE BLOCK IS PLACED ON THE CLOTH AND REGISTERED IN ITS PRECISE POSITION BY HAND AND THEN THE DYE IS APPLIED TO THE CLOTH WITH A BLOW FROM A HAMMER. THERE ARE OFTEN SLIGHT VARIATIONS DUE TO CHANGES OF PRESSURE ON THE BLOCKS OR MIS-REGISTRATIONS THAT ARE VALUED AS PROOF OF THE HANDICRAFT INVOLVED.

BLOTCH - THE NAME GIVEN TO A GROUND COLOR. IT CAN BE APPLIED IN SCREEN PRINTING BY USING A SEPARATE SCREEN, OR A LIGHT COLOR CAN BE APPLIED BY PUTTING THE CLOTH THROUGH A TINT BATH (AS IN "TEA-STAIN" FABRIC GROUNDS). THE MOTIF COLORS SCREENED ON TOP ARE AFFECTED BY THE TINT.

COLOR CHIPS- THE NAME GIVEN TO SQUARES OF COLOR INDICATING THE COLOR OF EACH SCREEN. ACTS AS PART OF THE INSTRUCTION TO PRINTERS.

CONVERSATIONAL- A DESIGN WITH RECOGNIZABLE OBJECTS AS MOTIFS. (E.G. ANIMALS, TELEPHONES, HANDS, SKULLS)

CROQUIS- A SKETCH OR REPRESENTATION OF AN IDEA FOR A DESIGN WHICH HAS NOT BEEN FULLY REALIZED OR PUT INTO REPEAT. ALSO USED TO DESCRIBE A TEMPLATE TO CREATE FLAT SKETCHES.

DAMASK- A CLOTH WOVEN BY A JACQUARD LOOM WHERE A PATTERN OF ORNAMENTAL MOTIFS IS WOVEN IN ONE COLOR. THE WEAVE GIVES A TONE-ON-TONE EFFECT TO THE CLOTH.

DIRECTIONAL - A PATTERN THAT ONLY WORKS FROM ONE DIRECTION (E.G. CAT HEADS FACING UP)

ENGINEERED - A MOTIF OR GROUP OF MOTIFS THAT ARE DESIGNED TO FIT A SPECIFIC SHAPE - LIKE A SLEEVE. THIS DESIGN IS NOT PUT INTO A REPEAT.

TEXTILE DESIGN GLOSSARY (CONT'D)

FALL-ON - THE AREA IN WHICH ONE SCREEN IS PRINTED ON TOP OF ANOTHER TO PRODUCE A NEW COLOR. AKA- TRAPPING. (E.G. RED FALLING ON YELLOW WILL YIELD AN ORANGE TRAP.)

FLORAL - A DESIGN USING FLOWERS OR OTHER NATURE ELEMENTS SUCH AS SEED PODS, LEAVES AND/OR MARINE PLANTS AS THE MAIN MOTIFS

FOULARD - SMALL SCALE PATTERNS WITH A BASIC BLOCK REPEAT USING SMALL-SCALE GEOMETRIC IMAGES.

GEOMETRIC - A MOTIF, PATTERN OR DESIGN DEPICTING ABSTRACT, NON-REPRESENTATIONAL SHAPES SUCH AS LINES, CIRCLES, ELIPSES, TRIANGLES, RECTANGLES AND POLYGONS.

HALF-DROP REPEAT - THE DESIGN WORKS BY BEING DROPPED HALF WAY DOWN THE FIRST AREA OF THE PATTERN. THIS RENDERS THE REPEAT MODULE A BIT MORE HIDDEN AND MORE INTERESTING WITH FEWER MOTIFS. IT ALSO AVOIDS THE SAME MOTIF APPEARING AT THE SAME LEVEL.

"OUTER-SPACES" - UNEVEN GAPS BETWEEN MOTIFS IN A DESIGN. AVOID IN YOUR LAYOUTS.

MOTIF - IDENTIFIABLE IMAGES OF A TEXTILE DESIGN.

REALISTIC - WHERE THE REPRESENTATION OF FORMS IS CLOSE TO REALITY.

CLOSED - A LAYOUT WHERE DESIGN MOTIFS ARE CLOSE TOGETHER. THERE IS LITTLE GROUND SHOWING.

OPEN - A LAYOUT WHERE MOTIFS ARE FAR APART. THERE IS MORE GROUND SHOWING (50% OR MORE).

REPEAT - THE METHOD OF CONSTRUCTING A DESIGN THAT FITS INTO A SPEC-IFIED FORMAT SO THAT IT CAN BE PRINTED ONTO AN INFINITE AMOUNT OF YARDAGE. THE DISTANCE BETWEEN IDENTICAL MOTIFS.

SQUARE - ALSO CALLED A BLOCK REPEAT. LIKE FLOOR TILES. THE REPEATING UNIT APPEARS DIRECTLY ON A HORIZONTAL PLANE TILING UP + DOWN, RIGHT + LEFT.

TWO-DIRECTIONAL - A LAYOUT THAT CONTAINS MOTIFS FACING 2 DIRECTIONS (E.G. CAT HEADS FACING BOTH UP AND DOWN) THIS TYPE OF LAYOUT SAVES FABRIC WHEN CUTTING PATTERNS

WHAT IS A CROQUIS?
THE WORD CROQUIS MEANS SKETCH
IN FRENCH. USE THESE FIGURES AS
A TEMPLATE FOR FLAT SKETCHES.
FIRST PHOTOCOPY THE CROQUIS.
THEN USE TRACING PAPER AND
YOUR RULERS + S-CURVES TO
CREATE SOME GARMENTS.

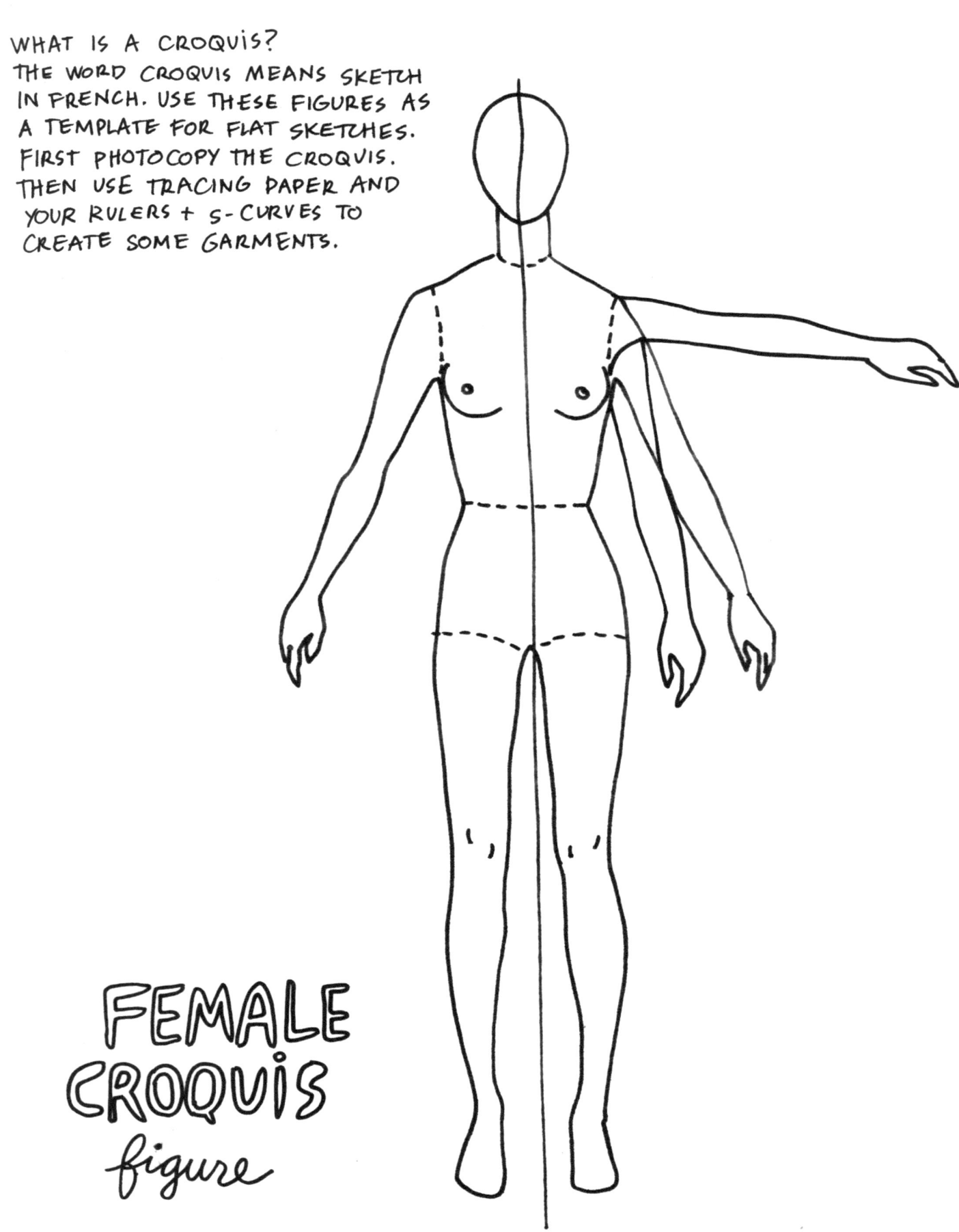

FEMALE
CROQUIS
figure

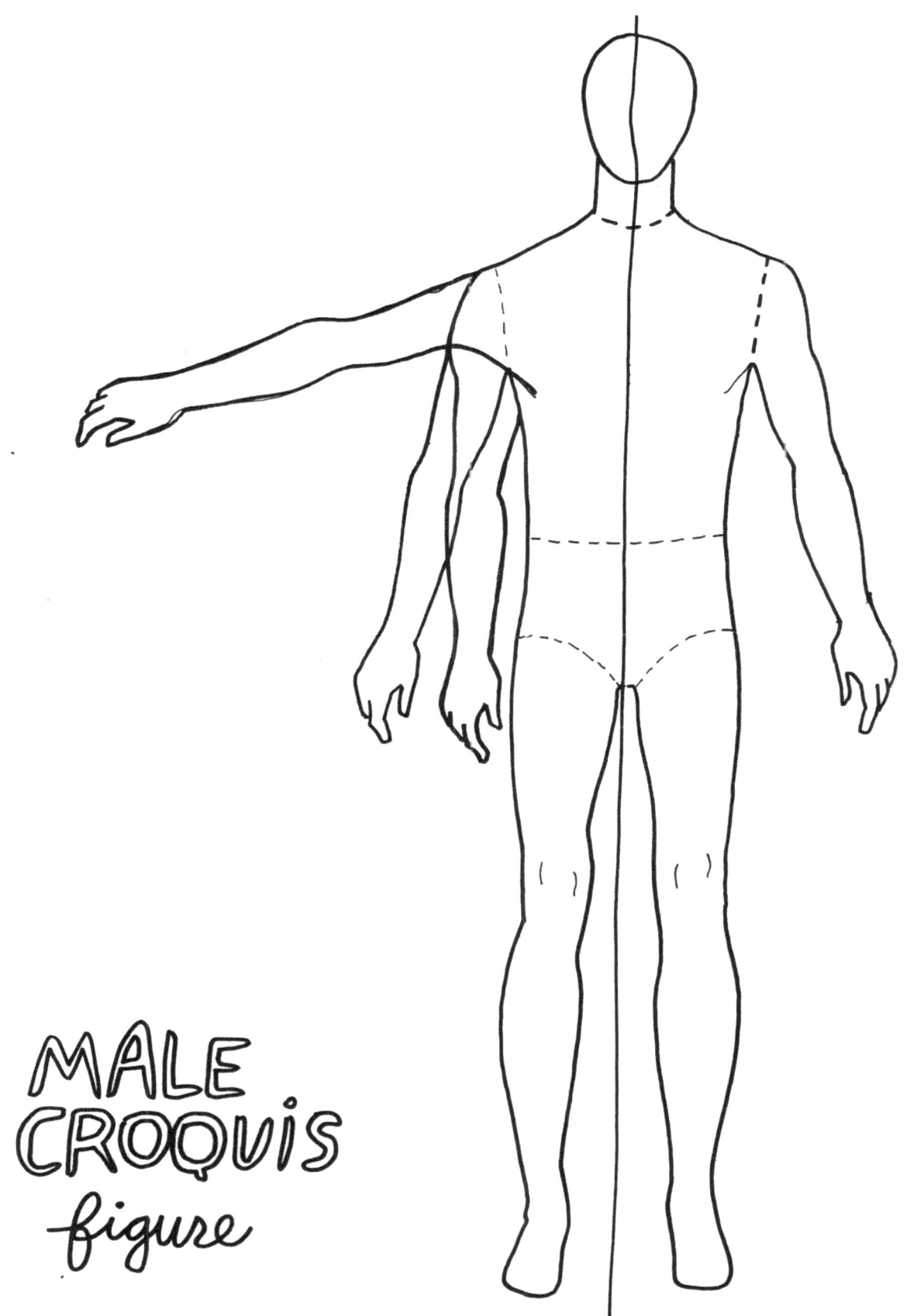

MALE
CROQUIS
figure

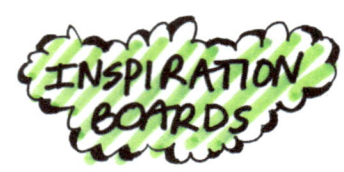

INSPIRATION BOARDS

* BEFORE WE EVEN BEGIN TO SKETCH GARMENTS, CHOOSE COLORS, PICK FABRICATIONS, DECIDE ON PRINT MOTIFS, OR DRAW FASHION FIGURES; LET US FIND A THEME THAT IS AT ONCE INTERESTING, EXCITING, MOTIVATING + FILLS US WITH WONDER. THIS WAY WE CAN CONTINUE TO BE INSPIRED FOR MANY MONTHS. NATURE, TECHNOLOGY, SCIENCE, TRAVEL, THE ARTS, FILM, MUSIC AND DANCE SERVE AS GOOD SOURCES FOR INSPIRATION.

1) ONCE YOU HAVE CHOSEN A THEME START YOUR RESEARCH. GO TO THE PICTURE COLLECTION AT THE LIBRARY + COLOR COPY AT LEAST 20 IMAGES. THE IMAGES SHOULD RANGE IN SCALE AND COLOR. (ALTERNATELY YOU CAN SCAN THE IMAGES DIRECTLY INTO PHOTOSHOP. SEE APPENDIX) ALSO, GO THROUGH YOUR MAGAZINES + TEAR OUT PAGES RELATED TO YOUR THEME.

2) EITHER BY HAND USING SCISSORS OR USING THE LASSO TOOL, CUT INTERESTING SHAPES AROUND EACH IMAGE. DO NOT USE ALL SQUARE OR RECTANGULAR SHAPES TO COLLAGE. THIS BECOMES A BIT TOO GRID-LIKE + BORING.

☐ , ▭ ← NOT , BUT → ⬭ , ⬬ , ⬮ , ETC.

3) USE: THE LAYERS PALETTE - OPACITY CHANGES
FILTER < BLUR
OPACITY MASKS - MAKE A SELECTION
CLICK LAYER MASK ICON
USE THE WHITE/BLACK GRADIENT TOOL
TO CLICK AND DRAG
FROM LESS OPAQUE TO MORE
OPAQUE
} TO CREATE AN INTERESTING WORK OF ART. (THIS IS YOUR MOOD BOARD)

4) IF CREATING BY HAND, USE 11 X 17" ILLUSTRATION BOARD. YOU MAY HAVE TO CUT THE BOARD TO SIZE WITH AN EXACTO KNIFE. GLUE IMAGE WITH A GLUE STICK OR JADE BOOK-BINDERS GLUE.

PRINTING

OK, SO WE'VE DESIGNED AN ENTIRE COLLECTION OF GARMENTS, TEXTILE DESIGNS + A BEAUTIFUL COLOR STORY. HOW DO WE TRANSLATE OUR DIGITAL MASTERPIECES ONTO FABRIC?

1) VIA SCREEN PRINTING. WHAT IS THAT?
A FABRIC SCREEN STRETCHED ONTO A WOOD FRAME IS COATED WITH A PHOTO SENSITIVE EMULSION. THEN A FILM POSITIVE (BLACK INK ON ACETATE) OF THE DESIGN IS PLACED ON TOP OF A LIGHT BOX FACE UP. THE SCREEN IS PLACED ON TOP AND THE WHOLE BUSINESS IS EXPOSED TO LIGHT FOR A FEW MINUTES. THE BLACK AREAS OF THE DESIGN BLOCK THE LIGHT + THE EMULSION RETAINS ITS WATER SOLUBILITY. THE AREAS EXPOSED TO LIGHT WILL HARDEN. THE WATER SOLUBLE AREAS OF THE EMULSION WILL BE RINSED AWAY TO YIELD A STENCIL. INK CAN NOW BE PRESSED THROUGH THE SCREEN WITH A SQUEEGEE ONTO FABRIC OR PAPER.

2) VIA BLOCK PRINTING (SEE APPENDIX PG. iv)
HERE WE ARE CUTTING THE RELIEF OF THE POSITIVE IMAGE INTO LINOLEUM OR WOODEN BLOCKS.

3) DIGITAL PRINTING
DIGITAL PRINTING GIVES US THE WIDEST RANGE AS FAR AS COLOR GOES. WE CAN HAVE BEAUTIFUL PHOTOGRAPHIC AND TONAL EFFECTS AS PART OF THE DESIGN.

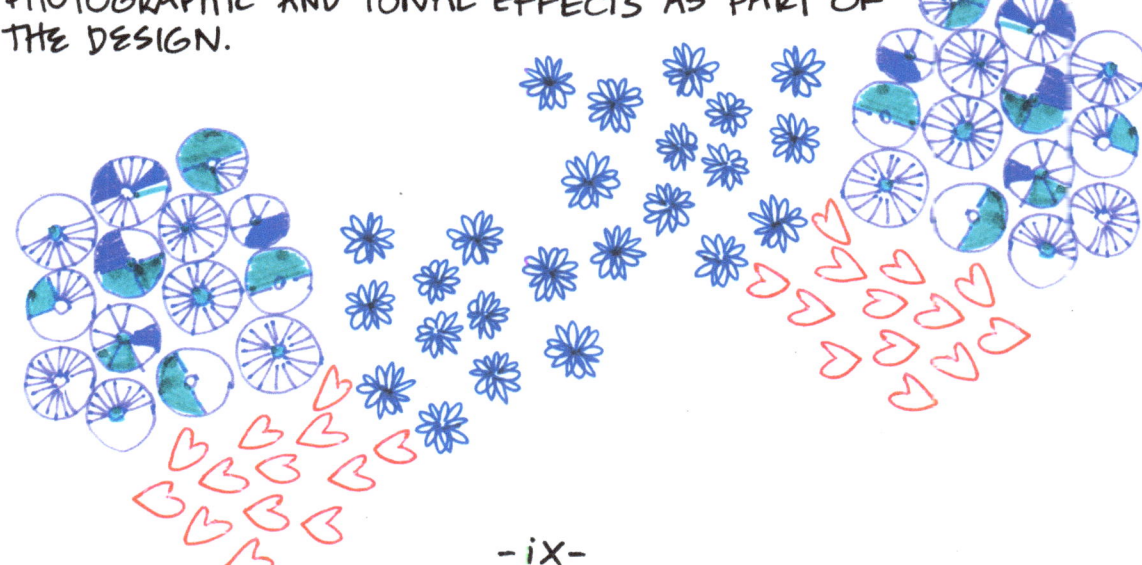

BIBLIOGRAPHY

HERE ARE SOME BOOKS IN MY PERSONAL LIBRARY THAT I REFER TO ALL THE TIME. START WITH 1 BOOK YOU ARE DRAWN TO AND BUILD YOUR COLLECTION SLOWLY OVER TIME. GOOD BOOKS ARE LIKE GOOD FRIENDS!

TEXTILES, CONCEPTS AND PRINCIPLES
   VIRGINIA ELSASSER; 2005, FAIRCHILD PUBLICATIONS

FASHION ILLUSTRATION NEXT
   LAIRD BORRELLI; 2004, CHRONICLE BOOKS

FROM PENCIL TO PEN TOOL
   ARMSTRONG, IVAS, ARMSTRONG; 2006, FAIRCHILD BOOKS

FAIRCHILD'S DICTIONARY OF TEXTILES
   PHYLLIS G. TORTORA; 1996, FAIRCHILD BOOKS

HANDBOOK OF WEAVES
   G.H. OELSNER; 1952, DOVER BOOKS

ILLUSTRATING FASHION
   STEVEN STIPELMAN; 1996, FAIRCHILD BOOKS

9 HEADS, A GUIDE TO DRAWING FASHION
   NANCY RIEGELMAN; 2000, 9 HEADS MEDIA

ADOBE ILLUSTRATOR FOR WINDOWS + MAC (VISUAL QUICK START)
   WEINMAN + LOUREKAS; 2009

ADOBE ILLUSTRATOR CLASSROOM IN A BOOK
   ADOBE PRESS; 2009

SAMPLE IMAGES

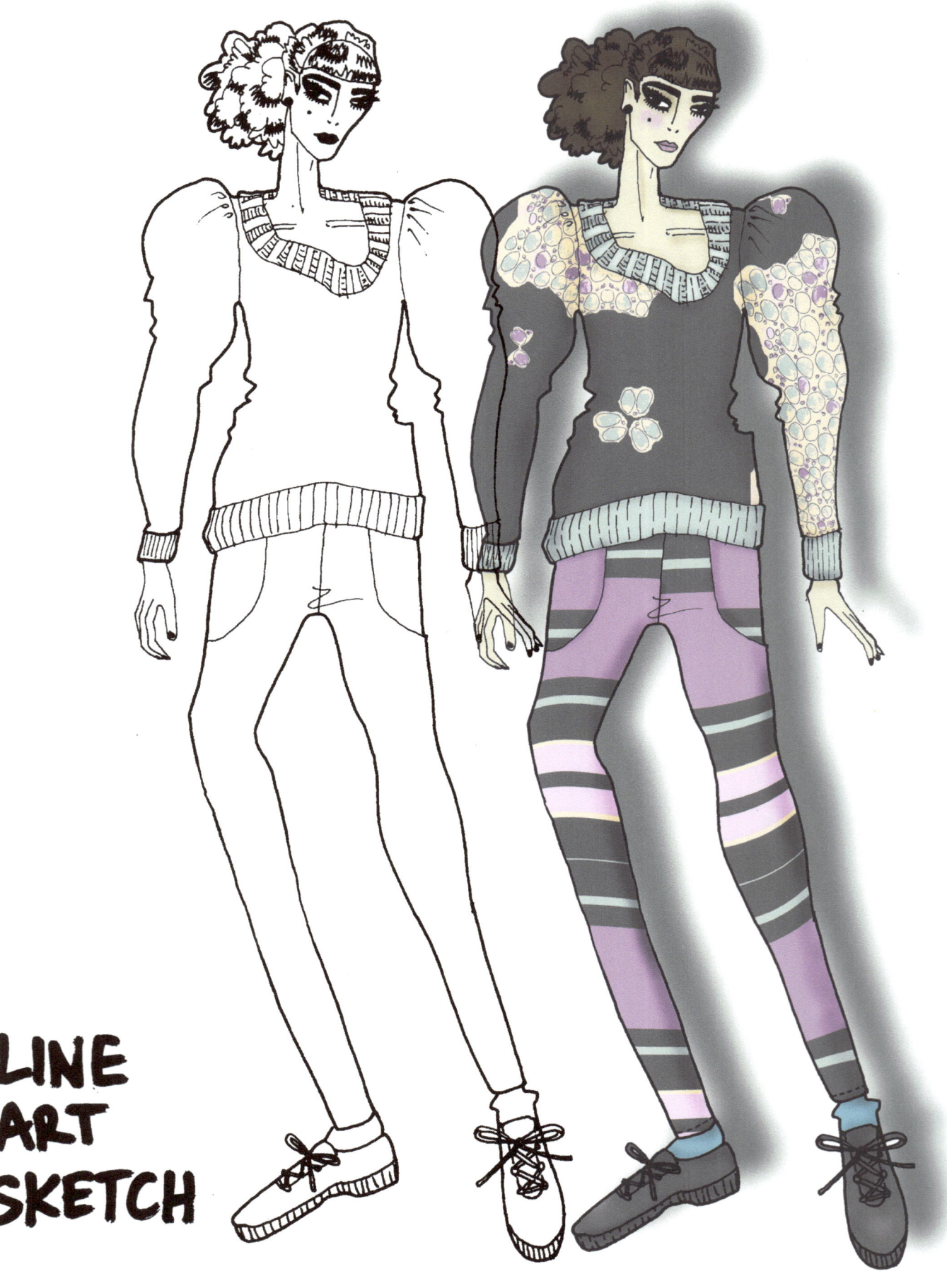

LINE
ART
SKETCH

MOOD BOARD
INSPIRATION: OWLS

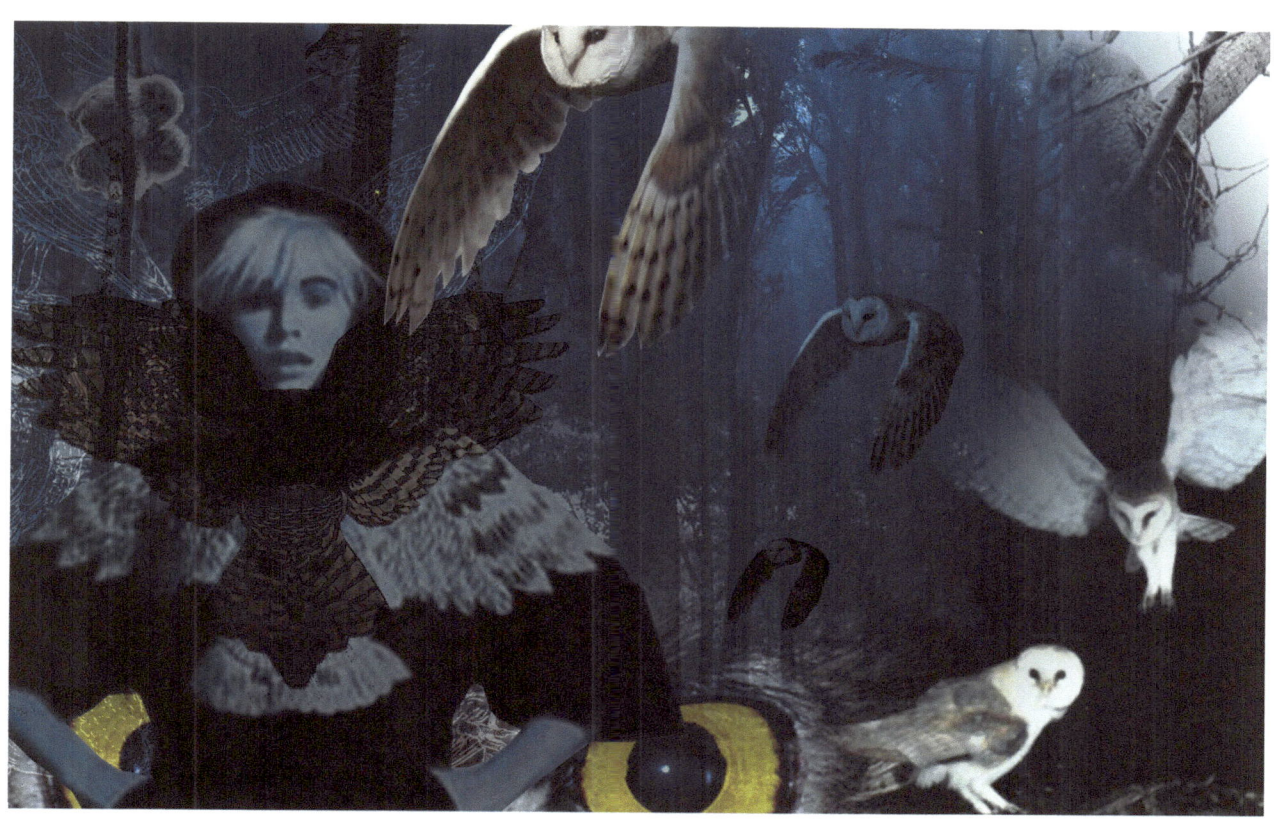

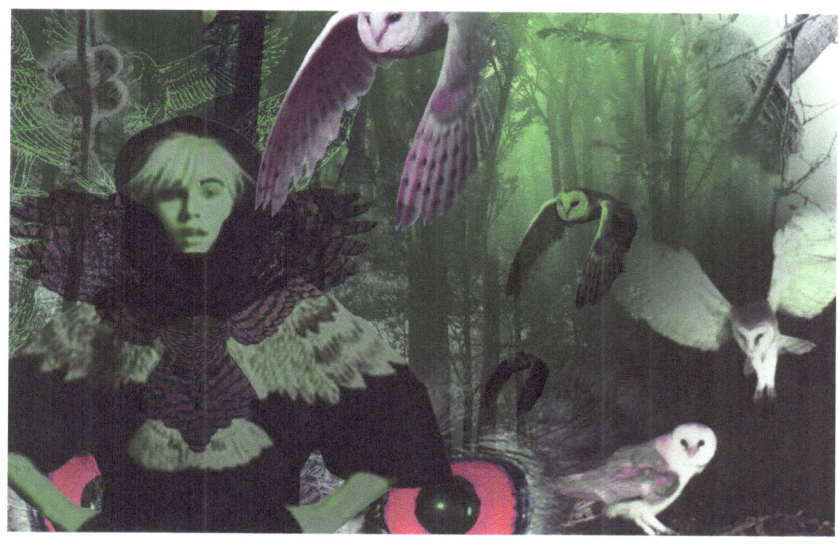

COLOR PALETTES
DELIVERY 1

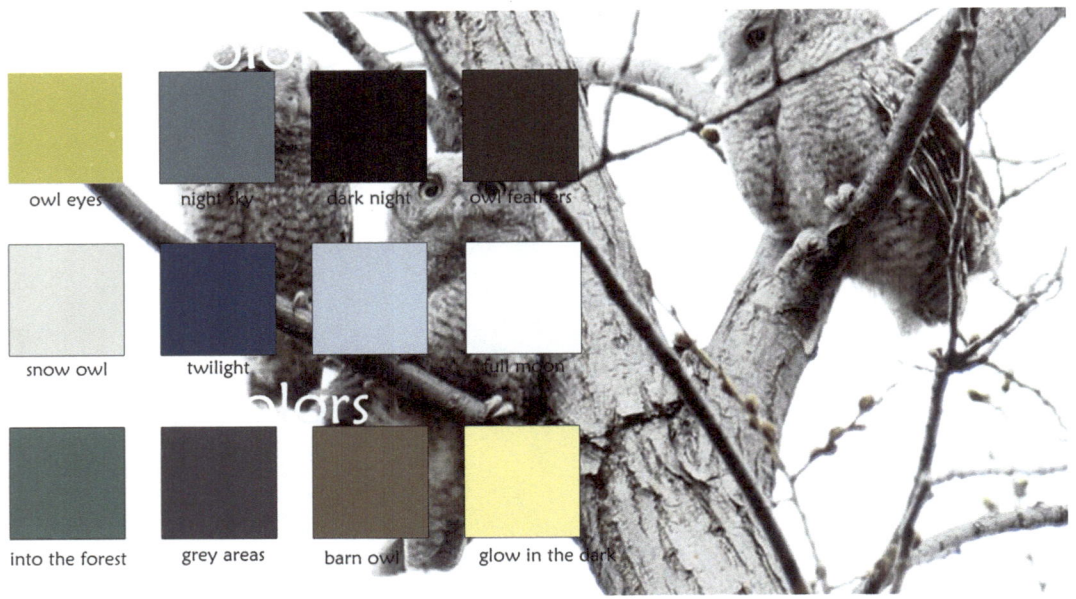

owl eyes   night sky   dark night   owl feathers

snow owl   twilight   full moon

into the forest   grey areas   barn owl   glow in the dark

DELIVERY 2

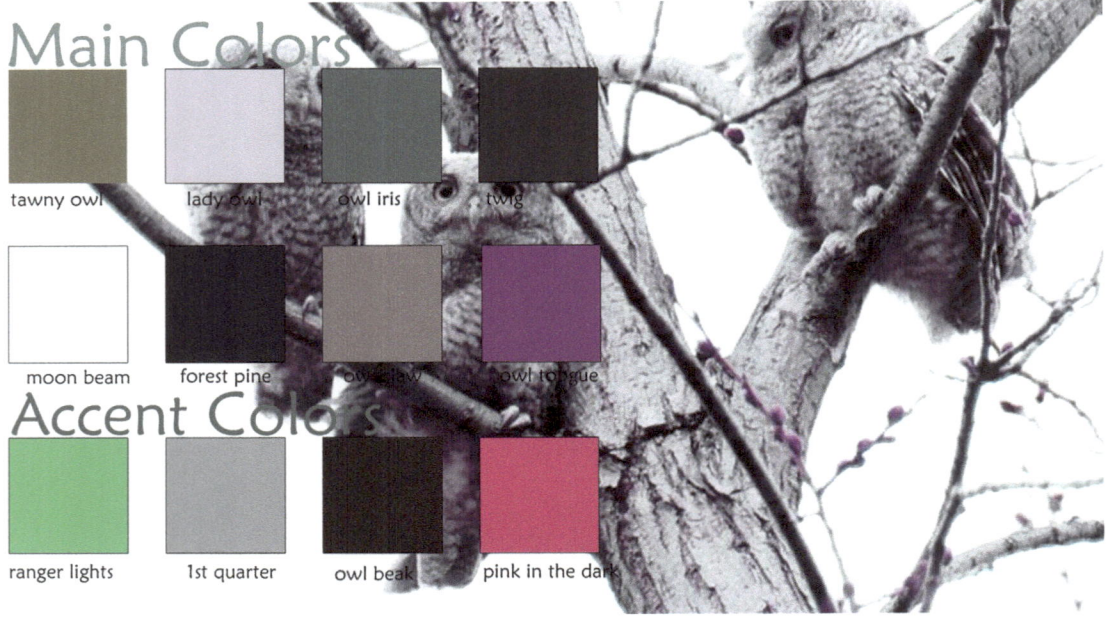

Main Colors

tawny owl   lady owl   owl iris   twig

moon beam   forest pine   owl jowl   owl tongue

Accent Colors

ranger lights   1st quarter   owl beak   pink in the dark

textile designs

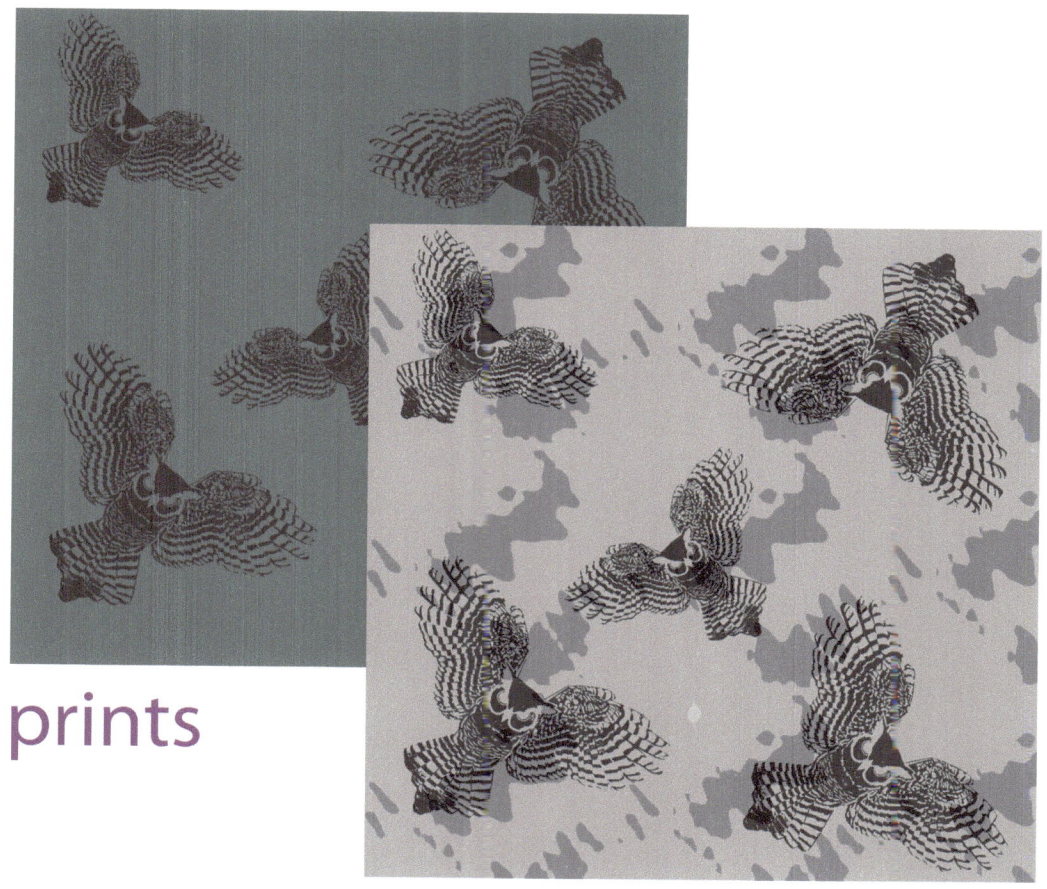

prints

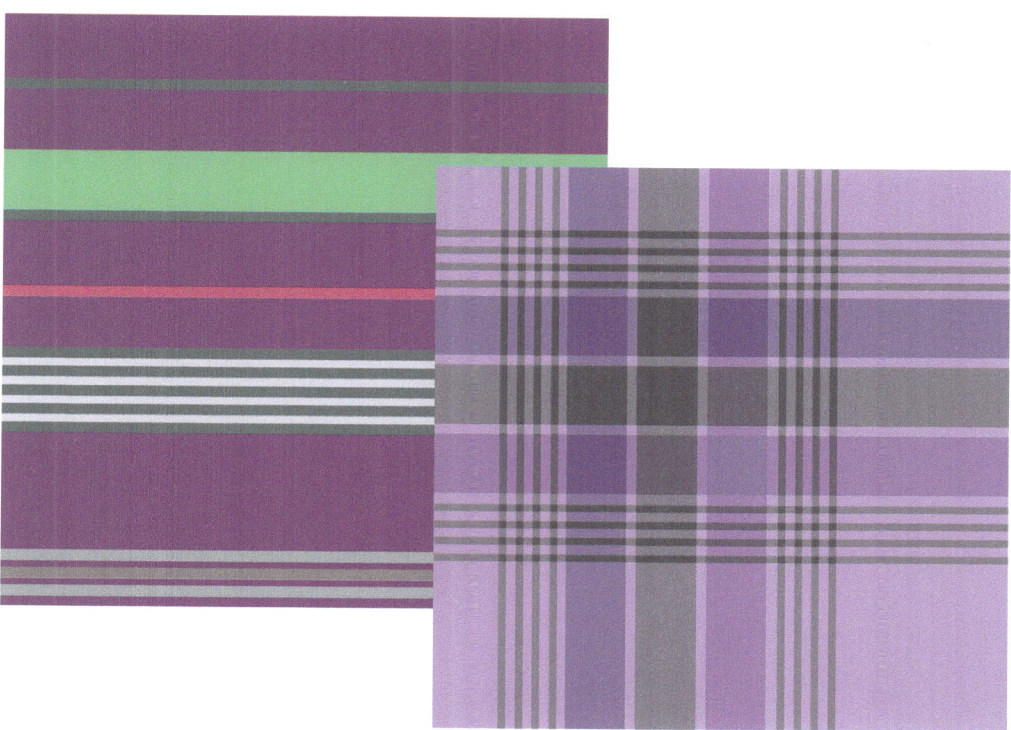

plaids + stripes

LAYOUT
DELIVERY ONE

NOTES

NOTES

NOTES

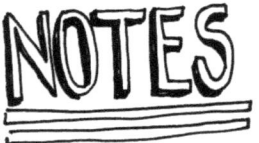

NOTES